# A Very Great City One Day

Roger Pegrum

First published in 2019 by Barrallier Books Pty Ltd

Registered Office: 35-37 Gordon Avenue, West Geelong, Victoria 3220, Australia.

www.echobooks.com.au

Copyright © Roger Pegrum

Author: Pegrum, Roger

Title: A Very Great City One Day: reflections of a Canberra architect

ISBN: 9780648355267 (Hardcover)

 A catalogue record for this book is available from the National Library of Australia

Book design by Peter Gamble, Canberra. Cover by Luke Bicevskis
Set in IBM Plex Serif Light, 11/14.

One of these days this will be a very great city if nothing happens to it.

*Henry Adams*
*Washington DC*
*November 1877*

# Contents

| | |
|---|---|
| Foreword | vii |
| Author's Note | xiii |
| Singapore to Narrabundah | 1 |
| The Swinging Sixties | 31 |
| Private Practice 1 | 65 |
| The Sydney Years | 95 |
| Back to Canberra | 117 |
| Selling Dreams | 151 |
| Postscript | 199 |

# Foreword

It is an honour and a privilege to have been asked to write a foreword for this book by Roger Pegrum. It is, on the one hand, an absorbing account of a life well lived (if far from complete) as an architect, thinker and organiser of spaces, and a person who has had and still, *deo volente,* will continue to have a profound effect on thinking about the national capital, its look, its feel, its setting in a very Australian landscape, and about how design can be harnessed to complement and allow the enjoyment and economical use of the people, the administrators and the people who live in the city and its suburbs.

He can be confident and proud of his role and his record as an important player in the creation of the living national capital. He can be proud of his public buildings and model landscapes, of the many houses he designed for the needs of citizens of the community, the work that he led on projects big and small as a government, finally as the government architect, of his role as a teacher, a writer and a promoter at local, national and international levels of the highest standards of building and design. It has contributed to better building, a better community and a better Australia.

But Roger is not given to self-satisfaction or complacency, but unease—a fear that many of the ideas, ideals and standards that actuated so much of the city he loves may be slipping. It is an alarum—a warning that the city is a continuing project still able to be compromised by bad planning, bad design, bad architecture and bad building. It's particularly at risk right now by a propensity for the second-rate, the short term, the quick fix and a quick profit. We want

*View from Mt Ainslie*
c.1936
Frozen in Time
Gallery

instead, from territorial as well as national guardians, the conditions for a dynamic, thoughtful and people-oriented polity living as privileged members of a city that is, or should be, the model and envy of other Australians and of the world. We have always had some barbarians inside the city walls, but they have never been so numerous or so dangerous.

It was said of another great architect that if you seek his monument, one should look around. Roger Pegrum has made his mark on many parts of the national capital, and even on the national insignia. I see one footprint every day, as I look past my front garden to Anzac Parade. That grand Avenue was of course conceived by Walter Griffin but, like his lake, it was not realised for nearly half a century. The lake was filling and the Kings and Commonwealth Avenue bridges were defining the land axis. Roger worked with William Holford at the National Capital Development Commission to make Anzac Parade what has been called the most considered street in Canberra. One of Roger's special contributions was the plan for the lighting of the parade— the string of pearls which makes the plan sing by night as much as by day, creating a vista as recognisable to most Australians as the Opera House or the Sydney Harbour Bridge. The lights have since been replaced, if to a similar type of design—and they, and the original, are now so ensconced in the national imagination that is almost impossible to imagine it otherwise.

This book shows how Roger came to be so well-equipped in his art and his craft, and in the small picture and the details as much as the broad scheme and its underlying ideas. He arrived in Canberra as a young boy, living in far-flung Narrabundah, and attending at first Telopea Park School and later Canberra High School, itself one of Canberra's finest buildings and now the School of Art at the Australian National University. His father was an engineer who helped develop the city's water supply and imbued in his twins— both to be architects—not only a sense of design, and of simple elegance, but also of practicality and durability. The large town in which Roger grew up may not yet have had its lake, but the urban area, as it was, was already being laid out along the lines of the Griffin plan, no doubt an experience reinforced by mostly walking and cycling, as well as by experiencing both its setting in, and its companionship with, the Australian bush. He is, in short, steeped in the broad plan of Griffin, whether as conceived by Griffin himself, or by those who were its stewards, and by those who lived in what was being achieved and what was being imagined of it. And that embraced additional theories of a garden city, of a bush capital, of bare hills, of extensive tree and shrub plantings, of human-scale public buildings, locally organised community facilities, and later, of town centres and the Y-plan. In all of it—if now under some threat because of unwise development—was the notion that the national capital could set standards in how ordinary Australians anywhere could live economically, enjoy enormous physical, social and economic amenity, on suburban land and in houses an ordinary young family could afford. For Roger, that innate understanding of the plan was increased by close scholarship, and not only in how Canberra came to be selected as the site for a capital city; how the Griffin plan won an international prize for urban design, and how the development of the city, its interim parliament house and early public service offices started, then stuttered until Sir Robert Menzies re-installed some momentum in the mid-1950s.

This book tells of his studies in Sydney, his early work in planning and developing public buildings and public places—in Canberra and elsewhere—whilst in the service of the then Works Department, his early ventures into private architecture, shift back to scholarship and teaching about architecture and design, his return as the government architect, and return to designing and building for industry, for families, and, still, government. He discusses details of some of his ideas, arguments won and lost, and the politics and the players as the city developed. It is no mere record of jobs performed. Whether in fitting his designs into the needs of clients, including the characteristics and peculiarities of people for whom he designed houses, or in seeking to adapt to new building and design techniques without becoming victim to the merely cheap, the tawdry and the second-rate. Many of the arguments he recounts echo today, and the effects of some of the arguments he lost are reflected in buildings without a sense of place or purpose, character in keeping with the site, or sympathy to its neighbourhood and social and physical environment. Clients, even governments, do not always have unlimited resources, and there are other constraints. None call for lowered standards, reduced quality or visual or environmental blight on the landscape. Still less do they call for a reduced integrity of planning process, a want of public consultation, or a land release program devised for maximum public revenue and incidental private impoverishment.

We should nourish Canberra's own special qualities and character and not try to be like somewhere else, he exclaims in this book. 'We can afford to wait for the glass to fill; people should come to Canberra because it is a very fine city, not because it is very big. And the quest to import vibrancy is a dangerous distraction. People will come from near and far and gather in places they like and where they feel safe. What Jane Jacobs called 'the safety of the streets and the freedom of the city' will in due course bring us the urban intensity, street markets, fiestas and fun. In the meantime, we can do something about our terribly boring streetscape and skyline, where no space has been wasted on lanes and alleyways and forecourts, everyone building to the same permitted height.'

Anyone with experience of the development of this city will be aware of the controversies of the past, and some of the issues still left undone for future resolution, if, we hope, in sympathy and broad if perhaps imaginative conformity with the great planning principles that have given us the city we have. Anyone familiar with that history knows that there is nothing new about some sense of crisis and of having reached important turning points, with the risk of bad outcomes. There's a tendency on the part of the advocates of some of the present slippage to accuse all those who would defend the legacy and the ideals of being simply opposed to development. That is not the case. But everyone in Canberra—politician, planner, designer, or simple citizen or consumer is, or ought to be, a steward of the great idea. If we don't get things right now, and if we do not uphold standards for the future, it may take decades, even centuries, to get it right again. That's not a call for panic, but for mature and deliberate decision-making.

Jack Waterford
Canberra
November 2018

# Author's Note

I have watched Canberra grow up as it has grasped the opportunities and taken on the responsibilities of a national capital city. It has been an exhilarating journey, slow at first and with both remarkable growth spurts and periods of relative calm. At every point it has been clear that it is not an ordinary city. Today, after 100 years of life, it is poised to be one of the great cities of the modern world.

Canberra has shaped the lives of many people. It is a beautiful place to live and work, conceived in confidence and hope and brought to life by the courage and commitment of many thousands of people. I am fortunate to have known some of the best and brightest among us, those who have come to Canberra and made their mark in planning and landscape and in all fields of design. They are people I have admired and whose dreams I have shared.

From time to time I have 'left home', as people have always done, but Canberra has always brought me back. This is a story of my life in the bush capital and the many ways in which the city, its people and its setting have influenced me.

I saw this project originally as a personal memoir, mainly for family members and a few close friends. However, it gradually came to include some broad observations about the theory and practice of architecture, the challenges of producing 'good' architecture within a bureaucratic framework, and the planning crossroads that Canberra is currently facing.

As a result, some friends and former colleagues convinced me there might be a wider audience for this book. I hope they are right.

The assistance and encouragement of a number of good friends is gratefully acknowledged. I am particularly indebted to Chris Freeman who has read many drafts of the text and has supplied creative support over a long period of time. Comment and corrections have been generously provided by Tony Blunn, David Evans, Grahame Crocket and Tony Morphett, and I have relied on the love and good sense of my wife Annabelle in telling the story accurately.

I have also received sound and helpful advice from Ian Donald and Georgia Leak at Barrallier Books. I thank Peter Gamble for his creative attention to the design of the book and Luke Bicevskis for his wonderful cover. I am grateful to the staff of the National Library of Australia, the National Archives of Australia and Parliament House and to Antoinette Buchanan and Kelly Tuckerman at the ACT Heritage Library for their assistance in assembling the many excellent illustrations.

Roger Pegrum
Canberra
March 2019

*planting near provisional Parliament House c.1936*
National Library of Australia

# Singapore to Narrabundah

*The Children of our Children*

When I first saw Canberra I was just ten years old and the city was not much older. Our family arrived by train from Sydney on the first weekend in October 1948 and we moved into a new three-bedroom red brick cottage at the top of McKinlay Street in Narrabundah, at that time almost the southernmost street in Canberra. The population was then around 15 000. The city was divided into two incomplete districts north and south of the Molonglo River, which flooded regularly and reinforced the image of Canberra as not one town but two. Formal landscaping and avenue planting was underway, but the majority of the trees in the city were still quite small and the climate was accordingly severe, with frosty winters and harsh westerly winds. Residential areas were well laid out with wide streets and generous public parks. Free-standing 'government houses', soundly built on large blocks, were allocated to public servants and their families transferred to Canberra and these outnumbered private houses several times over. Single men and women who came to Canberra lived in one of the many boarding houses and hostels scattered across town. When our first winter came, we all learned first-hand that water pipes on the outside of buildings freeze and explode overnight.

It was a time of growing regional and national confidence and expansion. Creative attempts to meet the post-war demand for housing in Canberra included prefabrication and the importation of timber barracks from military bases. There was a recognisable community spirit with local sporting fields and many social clubs. On the south side of town was a cinema and nearby swimming pool, there was a golf course on the river flats behind the Albert Hall, baby health centres in almost every suburb and small but fine churches on both sides of the river. Only twenty years earlier, the Federal Capital Commission had found it necessary to assure public servants transferred from Melbourne that every effort would be made to 'secure the comfort of officers and their families ... the conditions of life at Canberra will be a distinct contrast from the conditions of life in Melbourne but once the break is over ... it will be found by all that the change is for the good'.

There were no footpaths and few sealed roads in the brand-new suburbs and we had to plant potatoes to break up the clay soil but we all mucked in and loved every bit of it. When one day our street was tarred and sealed we were given the day off school. The milkman delivered our milk with a big ladle into a billycan my father had scalded the night before. It was my job to remove the water that collected at the bottom of the icebox and we liked to watch the iceman come around the back of the house late in the day with his giant calipers and an immense block of ice. My parents bought rugs for the bedrooms and living room and stained the bare wooden floors black around the edges. Ceilings were high at nine feet (2.7 metres) and I would have been grateful for that because I had the top bunk in a small bedroom I shared with my twin brother Tony. There was a chip heater for the bath and a copper tub in the laundry, a fireplace in the living room and a Kookaburra solid fuel stove and a meatsafe in the kitchen. A greengrocer's truck brought around fresh food and vegetables twice a week. We planted fruit trees in the front and back gardens and we had a compost heap and a push mower to cut the grass on an immense nature strip. We all rode bicycles to work or to school and as far as Pine Island and the Cotter River at weekends.

Canberra was certainly raw when we arrived, but it promised to be a fine place to live. It did not occur to me then to ask how this quiet valley came to be the capital city of Australia. Nor did I realise the impact Canberra was to have on all aspects of my life and how attached I would become to this beautiful place.

The origins of Canberra as our national capital city and seat of government are now well known. On 1 January 1901, after a lengthy and at times a difficult courtship, the six British colonies of New South Wales, Victoria, Queensland, Tasmania, South Australia and Western Australia consummated a carefully arranged federation to bring security and prosperity to all Australians. New South Wales, 'the mother colony', pressed its claims to host the Parliament of the Commonwealth of Australia in Sydney. Melbourne, the capital of Victoria, younger than Sydney but with the confidence of great wealth from the gold rushes of the 1870s, said that it would not object to the seat of government being somewhere in New South Wales provided it was not too close to Sydney. The founding fathers left it to the new Commonwealth Parliament to settle on its permanent home. The Constitution said only that the federal city must be at least one hundred miles from Sydney and that the Parliament would sit at Melbourne 'until it meet at the seat of government'.

In its search for a federal territory of its own, the young Australia would have been aware of the travails of the United States a century before, when the Congress had perambulated about New York, Philadelphia and six other cities before settling on the Potomac. The Parliament would also have been keen to avoid the troubles following the union of Upper and Lower Canada, when Quebec, Montreal and Toronto had each claimed the right to house the federal government, so that Queen Victoria had to step in with the compromise site of Ottawa. Australia seemed determined to choose the site for its federal city as soon as possible and to do so without calling for outside help. The Blue Mountains was the preferred site of the New South Wales government but Victoria said that was too close to Sydney. A fierce 'battle of the sites' focused on the south-east corner of New South Wales. The other states generally refrained from what they saw as an east coast squabble. If the capital was to be in the bush, they said, it would for most of the year be 'a place of magnificent distances and deadly dullness' where 'melancholy lunatics could live and thrive'.

An optimistic view of Australia's future capital city was given by King O'Malley, who had been elected to the first federal parliament to represent Tasmania, the smallest State

THE FUTURE AUSTRALIAN CAPITAL ON THE SNOWY.
*A forecast of Dalgety half a century hence.*

*Lionel Lindsay's drawing of a federal capital city at Dalgety NSW*
Lone Hand 1 April 1908

of the Commonwealth. In October 1903, O'Malley summed up his vision for a new city on the cool ranges, away from the frenzy of the warmer coastal cities:

> Cold climates have produced the greatest geniuses ... how big is Scotland, whose sons are all over the earth? How big is the State of Maine? That State is not as big as Bombala and yet it gave birth to Longfellow. The Snowy River is fed by Heaven from the eternal snows of the mountains. In the very beginning the Garden of Eden was laid out to the eastward ... this is the first opportunity we have had of establishing a great city of our own. I hope that the site selected will be Bombala and that the children of our children will see an Australian federal city that will rival London in population, Paris in beauty, Athens in culture and Chicago in enterprise.

With a speed impossible to match today, the Commonwealth Parliament sitting in Melbourne took only a handful of years to settle on a site for a permanent seat of government and an Australian federal territory. The site selected in 1908 in the Yass-Canberra district was about one hundred and fifty miles from Sydney and offered clean air, a good water supply, a bracing climate and a fine setting for the capital city. Prime Minister Andrew Fisher moved quickly to find the best possible site in the chosen district. He borrowed surveyor Charles Scrivener from New South Wales, instructing him to find a site for 'a beautiful city occupying a commanding position with extensive views and embracing distinctive features which will lend themselves to the evolution of a design worthy of the object, not only for the present but for all time'. The government decided that the design of the city would be determined by an international competition, which it was said would attract 'hundreds of young, progressive and up to date professional men ... they have reputations to make'. Entrants were told that the city would be the 'official and social centre of Australia'. When entries closed early in 1912, 137 designs had been submitted.

Walter Burley Griffin was thirty-five years old when he was announced as the winner of the design competition. Born and raised in a quiet suburb of Chicago, Griffin had studied architecture at the University of Illinois. He graduated in 1899 and worked in the office of Frank Lloyd Wright, where he was much influenced by a man who would become one of America's foremost romantic architects. Also working in Wright's office at the time was Marion Mahony, one of the first women to graduate in architecture from the Massachusetts Institute of Technology and renowned for her talents as an artist and architectural delineator. In June 1911, only a short while after he had started work on his designs for Canberra, Griffin married Mahony.

Griffin's interests included broad aspects of landscape and community planning, not unlike the ideas being advocated in England by Ebenezer Howard in his arguments for garden cities. In his plan for Canberra, Griffin was able to develop these interests at a very large scale, and his designs were presented in a series of 14 exquisitely rendered panels prepared by Marion Mahony. The structure of his city plan was incorporated into two major lines; a water axis running south-east from Black Mountain along the line of a central lake and a land axis starting at Mount Ainslie and intersecting the water axis at a right angle. It was essential, said Griffin, that the buildings in any of the major groups—government, municipal, educational or military—be designed with proper attention to size and scale so that 'from any general viewpoint of the town [they] will work together into one simple pattern of fundamental simplicity'. With a 'horizontal distribution of buildings ... liberality in public space ... and directness and speed in communication between all points', Australia's capital city, he said, could avoid having its buildings 'stand on end as in congested American cities'.

The Griffin design for Canberra has fascinated planners for decades. It is generally acknowledged that a century of advances in town planning theory has not been able to improve on its simplicity and complexity. Peter Harrison, the first chief planner of the National Capital Development Commission, said that 'on paper anyone can understand it; on the ground it is hard to forget'. The greatest strength of the plan, said Harrison, is that it does not depend for its realisation on the construction of grand buildings. 'Buildings are made important'. said Harrison, 'not so much by their size, height or architectural magnificence, but by their setting. It is not an architectural composition but a landscape composition'. Much of the credibility of the Griffin design, it has been said, stems from a belief that it was 'the dream of a dreamer'.

*Federal Capital City Design Competition 1912 Walter Burley Griffin's winning design beautifully rendered on silk by his wife Marion Mahony*
National Archives of Australia

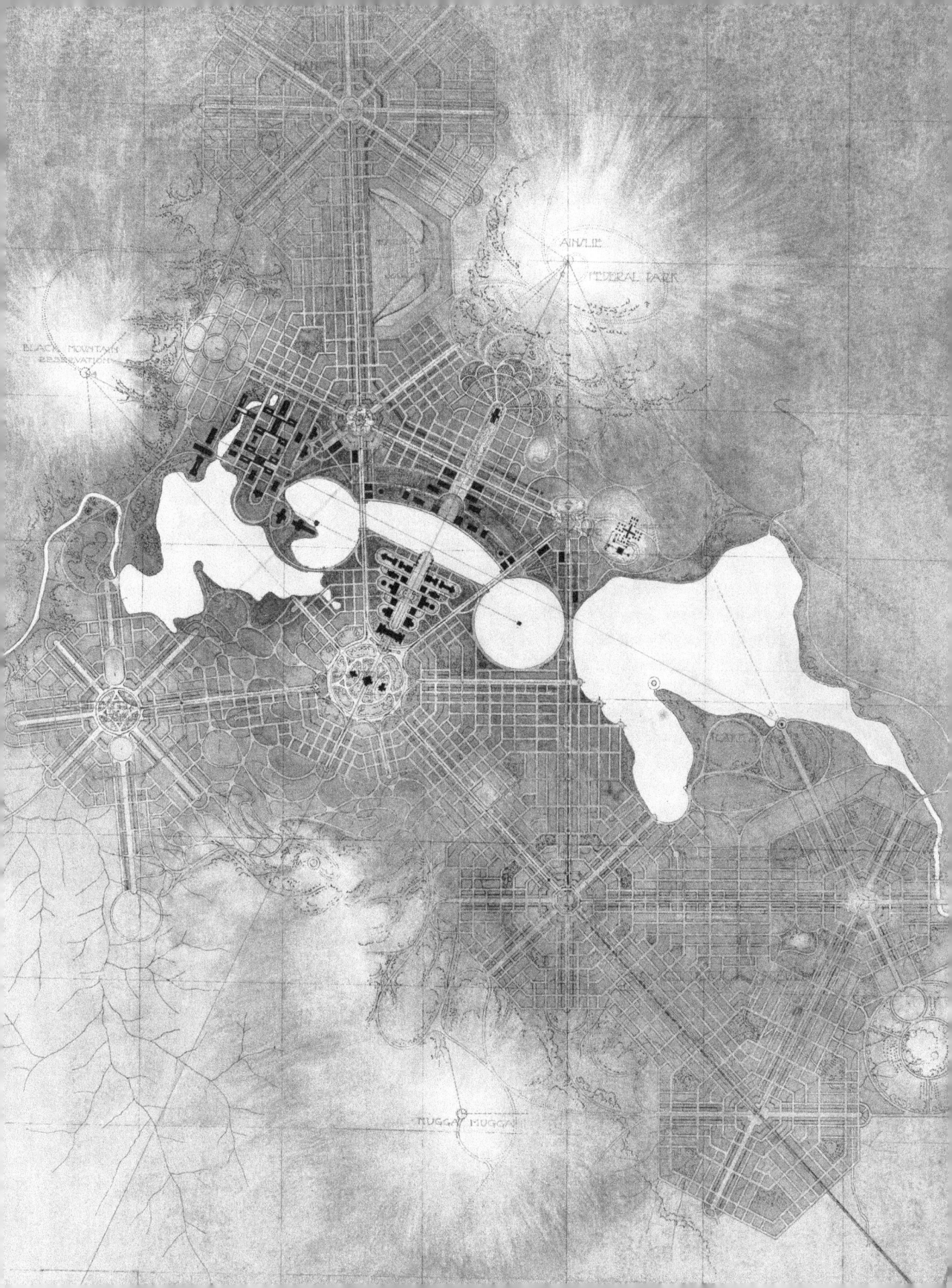

Edmund Bacon, the famed American urban planner, wrote in 1968 of Canberra's 'network of sweeping vistas, vast gulps of fresh air, superbly exciting and dynamic interactions between the peaks of hills and mountains and the movements of people … a great work of architecture'. Griffin would have been pleased to hear such fulsome praise; two months after his design was published it was suggested that he had 'been carefully reading books upon town planning without having much more than theoretical knowledge to go upon'. Daniel Burnham, who had laid out Chicago in the City Beautiful style after the great fire of 1871, did not live to see Griffin's design, but he too would have been pleased with its bold but subtle landscape plan which tied the city to the surrounding hills and valleys. 'Make no little plans', said Burnham when the competition for Australia's capital was announced, 'They have no magic in them to stir men's blood. Make big plans, aim high in hope and work, remembering that a noble, logical diagram once recorded will never die'.

The city was named and its foundation stone laid on 12 March 1913, when the Canberra valley was still a pleasant outback sheep station divided by the lazy Molonglo River. Griffin was brought to Australia and appointed Federal Capital Director of Design and Construction but his time in Australia was not peaceful. Constantly obstructed by politicians and the bureaucracy, Griffin left Canberra in 1919 never to return. In 1927, when the federal Parliament sat for the first time in Canberra, the city was described as 'a unique and interesting experiment … the modern and the picturesque blended into a composite and harmonious whole, cradled in a setting that for its purpose can have no peer'. Canberra today is to many minds the most Australian city of an immigrant nation, a cosmopolitan and egalitarian city-state reflecting the vast scale of the continent.

My father Harold Edward (known to everyone as Ted) Pegrum was born in Epping in Essex, England in 1908. He went to school at Roborough, a minor public school in East Sussex whose most famous alumnus was Alec Guinness. He studied as a civil and structural engineer at University College London and started work with Dorman

Long on the Isle of Wight. In 1934, he joined the office of the British Admiralty at Portsmouth and two years later was posted to the naval base at Singapore. He met my mother at Eastbourne, near Brighton, in the summer of 1935 and they were married at the parish church of St Mary Newington in April 1936, a month before sailing for Singapore. In 1938 my twin brother Anthony (Tony) and I were born across the Causeway in Johore Bahru in what was then the Federated Malay States, now Malaysia.

My mother, Eileen Florence Adams, was born in 1913 in Newington North in London and attended the Southwark Central School for Girls. In addition to the general classes of the secondary school curriculum, she studied French and a number of commercial subjects including shorthand, typewriting and bookkeeping. When she left the school, the headmistress wrote that 'Eileen Adams is well spoken, thoroughly straightforward and truthful ... her work is always praiseworthy ... she has the power of expressing her ideas clearly both in spoken and in written English and she is keenly interested in sport, in which she takes an active part'. After leaving school, she completed a course in business studies with distinction at the Pitman College in London. She joined the Ladies Polytechnic Athletics Club and travelled to athletic meets in many cities. She was at one time the third fastest woman in England over 100 yards. She trained at Crystal Palace with some of England's leading athletes, including Violet Webb, who went on to win Britain's first ever Olympic medal for women's athletics in the 4x100 metres relay in Los Angeles in 1932.

We left Singapore at the outbreak of the Second World War (I believe it was on the last ship not 'blacked out') and settled at Chatham in Kent, where my father was based at the naval dockyards on the River Medway. Tony and I went to Balfour Road School for a short time towards the end of the War, walking home each day with an eye on the barrage balloons put up to protect us from aerial bombardment. I have a very clear memory of the face of the pilot when a German aeroplane on fire crashed in the fields at the end of our street. From the summer of 1944, German rockets launched from Pennemunde flew over Chatham on their way to London. We spent many

*Singapore 1939*

*Balfour Road School
Chatham Kent 1946
Roger back row, teacher's
hands on shoulders
Tony front row,
fourth from the right*

evenings inside an Anderson air raid shelter which our father had buried in the back garden. We were fortunately inside the shelter when a flying bomb landed in the street, badly damaging our house and many others. We moved across City Way to Rochester, where we lived until our departure for Australia in 1948. My sister Carole was born in Rochester in 1946.

From late 1942 onwards, my father was involved in the design and construction of a number of secret military engineering projects in Scotland and on the south coast of England. These included the design and construction of very large concrete caissons for the Mulberry breakwaters that were floated across to Normandy for the invasion on D-Day 1944, and also Operation Pluto (Petrol Line Under The Ocean) which piped fuel under the English Channel to France. There has been renewed interest in these remarkable engineering achievements, some of which are described in the film 'A Harbour goes to France'. I knew very little about our father's wartime work until he gave an illustrated lecture on the Mulberry project to members of the Institution of Engineers about ten years after our arrival in Canberra. It was fairly certain, my father said at the time, 'that that no other single piece of engineering ever employed so many engineers at one time and in no other enterprise were they, and the general public, kept so much in the dark as to the ultimate object ... the remarkable nature of the harbours is that such a vast piece of work was done in such a fabulously short time'.

Construction of a safe harbour on an unguarded part of the French coast was essential for an Allied invasion of Europe,

*Mulberry Harbour: a Phoenix caisson moves out to sea April 1944*
Imperial War Museum

but a number of British engineers experienced in harbour work had been reluctant to be associated with 'anything so impracticable' saying that 'the inevitable failure to produce the goods in anything like the specified time would hold the entire profession up to ridicule'. But the idea grew into a determination and two fully equipped prototype ports were constructed inside Scottish lochs at Faslan and Stranraer and were tested successfully on the coast of Scotland in the spring of 1943. There was intense pressure to complete the work and mount the invasion during the following summer. Between June and September 1944, Germany launched some 7,500 flying bombs against England, one bomb every fifteen minutes, day and night, for eighty days. Six miles of caissons had to be ready in six months. 'A length of 200 feet was decided upon with a draft of about 20 feet and a breadth of 56 feet. Each caisson had a 'swim end' for lower resistance and steadiest towing ... altogether 212 caissons were made, of which 147 were ready for D-Day'. My father said that the caissons performed well—'the storm that started on D plus 12 and lasted for four days was quite unprecedented for the time of year ... none of the walls, which were nowhere more than 15 inches thick, collapsed from wave action and in no instance was there any sign of overturning ... the wind was at gale force for two days ... after the storm, the harbour at Arromanches was quickly returned to full efficiency as a port'.

In the years following the end of the War, it became clear to my parents that a better life for them and their children could be found away from England. Experienced architects and engineers were being sought for infrastructure works in Australia, Canada, South Africa and New Zealand and my father responded to advertisements from all of these countries. He was particularly attracted to a number of larger civil engineering projects in Australia, one of which aimed to increase the capacity of the dam built in 1915 on the Cotter River outside Canberra. In early 1948, he took the train up to London for an interview at Australia House, where he met with the Director from the South Australian office of the Commonwealth Department of Works. Not long afterwards, my father was offered a position as a structural engineer in the Australian Capital Territory regional office of the Department. His wartime experience with reinforced concrete and hydraulic engineering and an appreciation of tight timetables made him an ideal person for the proposed work. He was told there would be a house for his family in Narrabundah, which we all thought was a funny name for a place, and he brought home a booklet about the Australian language for us all to read. It seemed to me that we were about to set out on a great adventure.

We sailed from Tilbury on board RMS *Mooltan* in August 1948 and Tony and I turned ten somewhere east of Aden. The *Mooltan* was a refitted P & O steamer that had served as both a troop carrier and an armed cruiser during the War. I caused my parents great anxiety for most of the voyage by wandering all over the ship, particularly attracted to the engine rooms and other interesting spaces near the water line. In the manner of the time, the ship's passenger manifest said 'Mr H E Pegrum' on one line and on a second line 'Mrs Pegrum and 3 children'. On board with us was Grenfell Ruddock, an architect at the Department of National Development in Melbourne, who was on his way home from town planning studies in Liverpool under Professor William Holford (later Sir William and later still Baron Holford). Ruddock would come to Canberra ten years later as one of the first associate commissioners of the National Capital Development Commission and Holford would play a major role in the development of Canberra as an adviser to the Government and as a member of the National Capital Planning Committee. Also on board was John Scollay, an English architect who moved in with his family next door to us in Narrabundah. John joined my father at the Department of Works but moved on to be University Architect at the

*Cotter River and Dam c 1925*
State Library of Victoria

newly established Australian National University and then into a successful private practice in Canberra. In his later years, he was the first chief executive of the (then Royal) Australian Institute of Architects and moved into Stewart Murray's pleasant Mugga Way headquarters building when it opened in 1970.

My father started work immediately at the offices of the Department of Works in Barton and the first concrete was poured at the Cotter River in January 1950. When completed eighteen months later, the dam wall had been raised to 25 metres and this more than tripled Canberra's water storage. A much larger dam has now been built downstream and the original wall and my father's additions are lost forever under almost 50 metres of water. No mention was made at the launch of the latest dam of the 1915 dam nor my father's 1950 additions. How easy it is for today's business leaders and developers to believe that history started a week ago. On behalf of my father and all our pioneers, I was grateful to Steve Doszpot, who came to Australia from Hungary following the 1956 uprising, when he tabled a thoughtful tribute to my father and all the early engineers and builders of Canberra in the ACT Legislative Assembly in October 2011.

*54 McKinlay Street*
*Narrabundah*

By nature a conservative engineer and fascinated by building materials and mathematics, my father was widely respected in his profession. He welcomed challenge and innovation and loved living and working in the emerging Canberra. He transferred in 1956 to the Department of the Interior where he was responsible for approving the structural designs of many of the larger commercial projects in the city. Alan Roberts' excellent book *A Big Bold Simple Concept* talks of my father's role during construction of Roy Grounds' Academy of Science in Acton in the mid-1950s. My father was a firm but warm man who gently guided us as teenagers and young adults and was interested in everything that his children did. He retired in 1971 after a number of a heart attacks and he died too young in July 1979.

For more than twenty years my mother worked at the British High Commission on Commonwealth Avenue, where her talents in office management and her proficiency in written and spoken English were highly valued. She helped arrange the Queen's visit to Australia in 1954 and was a trusted assistant to a number of high commissioners. We knew little of the detail of her job but she did tell us she met Harold Macmillan, the first British Prime Minister to visit Australia, and also Margaret Thatcher, whom she said was 'a very nice lady'. She left the job with great reluctance in 1973 when she reached the mandatory retirement age of sixty. We celebrated her 100th birthday in style in 2013, the same year that Canberra celebrated its centenary. An active woman all

*My mother with visiting Prime Minister Harold Macmillan*
*British High Commission*
*Canberra February 1958*

*Molonglo River in flood February 1956 showing original bridge on Commonwealth Avenue. Institute of Anatomy left front, University House right front ACT Heritage Library (Canberra Times collection)*

her life, she enjoyed the company of her family and a shrinking number of close friends. Despite our protestations, she had a knee replacement at ninety-five and she died peacefully in Canberra when she was 104.

Tony and I attended Telopea Park Primary School where the headmaster, George Hurrell, introduced us to the sport of hockey. We played for local teams Barton and Old Canberrans for many years and joined the cubs and then the scouts and camped and canoed on the Cotter and Murrumbidgee rivers. On Saturday afternoons, we walked or rode our bikes to movie matinees at the Capitol Theatre in Manuka. Usually two films and a serial while we ate potato crisps with salt in a little blue twist of paper, sucked the brand-new lemonade ice-blocks and rolled Jaffas down the aisles. We were altar boys at St Paul's Church in Manuka, where we met Canberra's first resident architect, Ken Oliphant, and we learned to swim quick smart when we realised we were the only boys at school who could not. I was dux of Telopea Park School in 1950, receiving a gold medal at the Capitol Theatre from Charles Studdy Daley, who had been secretary to the Federal Capital Commission under Sir John Butters. Twenty years later, I was instrumental in C S Daley becoming the first honorary associate of the Australian Institute of Architects and we named a new award for housing after him.

After Telopea Park, Tony and I went to Canberra High School across the river in Acton, at the time the only public school in Canberra that took students through to the NSW Leaving Certificate. When it opened in 1939, the Art Deco style building was said by the *Canberra Times* to be 'as modern and well-equipped as any school in Australia … the last word in modern architectural design and comfort with the latest scientific educational equipment and ideas including audio and visual projection appliances'. The school had an excellent record at the Leaving Certificate and a serious-sounding motto *uno mente uno consilio*—(with one mind and one purpose) and it attracted young and committed teachers who were a bit funky and related well to the students. For five nights of the week our building was also a night school where men and women returned from the War and seeking undergraduate status at universities could study for the Intermediate and Leaving Certificates. The curriculum was broad and inclusive, with music and art and a wide range of languages including Latin, German and Japanese. We all had to take French because the headmaster F B Jones had written the definitive French grammar textbook and I took up German as well.

I was fortunate to have Terry Steinmetz as my English teacher. He loved the English language with a passion for the basics of grammar and syntax and lots of conjugations and declensions. My interest in writing comes most directly from my mother but also from the promise made by Steinmetz that the ability to write well would support us in all we do. Boys and girls alike took classes in cooking, woodwork and technical drawing. Our athletics coach was Max Landy, a snappily dressed fellow whose cousin John in 1954 became the first Australian to run a mile in less than four minutes. Tony and I took after our mother with our running, Tony doing well at sprints and me over longer distances.

*Canberra High School debating team 1956 L—R Neil McPherson, Elizabeth Spencer, Terry Steinmetz, Pat Geach, Roger Pegrum*

I was a member of the school debating team with Pat Geach, Neil Macpherson, Virginia Spate and Elizabeth Spencer for several years and was dux of each year except my final year in 1956. I matriculated to the University of Sydney determined that I would become an architect.

Tony and I rode our bicycles or took the bus to school each day, deviating sometimes to go past the Girls' Grammar School to chat up the girls. There were various ways to get from south to north across the Molonglo. Scott's Crossing ran from near the sculpture gardens of the present National Gallery across a causeway to Blundell's Cottage; when it rained heavily, this was the first crossing to go under. The next to go was Lennox Crossing, which ran from the back of the Albert Hall to the hospital at the Acton Peninsula. A timber trestle bridge carried the western half of Commonwealth Avenue over the Molonglo. The bridge moved around alarmingly when the river rose after heavy rains and when it wobbled too much we all got one or more days off school.

Behind the school and housing the heart of the legendary Australian racehorse Phar Lap and other grisly exhibits fascinating to all young boys and girls was the Institute of Anatomy, a wonderful Art Deco building with lovely Australian decorative elements and a beautiful internal courtyard. A small theatrette in the Institute was regularly used by our teachers for the more spectacular science demonstrations.

Across from the school playing fields were the arcaded Sydney and Melbourne Buildings, the only substantial buildings in the Civic Centre of Canberra. In April 1953, in our third year of high school, a fire destroyed the western half of the Melbourne Building, but it happened early on a Saturday morning so we missed all the fun. It was re-built within a year, in concrete and steel with a basement and fire sprinklers and was the first home of the Canberra University College.

Our school years passed pleasantly in this peaceful paradise. The city grew steadily with post-war immigration and there was intermittent building work both north and south of the Molonglo as some of the smaller federal departments and agencies were brought from Melbourne. By 1954, the population of Canberra was almost 40 000. The highlight of that year in Canberra (other than the defection of the Petrovs) was the visit of Queen Elizabeth II, the first reigning monarch to come to Australia. The two-month tour included a week in Canberra with opportunities every day to see the royals up close. The Queen opened Parliament on a rainy Monday morning in February and waved to us as she was driven around Manuka Oval. That afternoon a bus took us to a low rise near what is now the National Library where we held red, white and blue placards above our heads to keep off the rain and then (turning the placards over in some sort of unison) displayed for the Queen what we were told was a very large Union Jack. The next day the Queen unveiled the Australian-American Memorial at Russell Hill while the Duke of Edinburgh opened University House, and that evening the town went into party mode with spectacular fireworks in York Park.

By the time I had completed high school, I was in no doubt that I wanted to be an architect. In my choice of career, I was undoubtedly influenced by Canberra's early buildings and its slowly unfolding landscape. A small number of public buildings of modest architectural interest such as the Kingston Powerhouse and the Government Printing Office were major centres of employment. The fathers of many of my schoolmates worked in these places. We visited from time to time and I enjoyed watching the furnaces and the printing presses at work. At the middle of the rather empty valley was the provisional Parliament House and a matching pair of three-storey government office buildings. The nearby Hotel

Canberra and the Hotel Kurrajong provided accommodation for politicians and their staffs when Parliament was sitting. The Albert Hall on Commonwealth Avenue was a major venue for theatre and concerts and it had a huge movie projector. Its sprung floor made it popular for dances and it served as our school hall for my five years at Canberra High School.

The Albert Hall attracted the interest of the world in May 1954 as the venue for the Royal Commission on Espionage which enquired into the Petrov Affair and Soviet activities in Australia generally. The city's only public library was a lovely stone-faced three-storey building on Kings Avenue built in 1935 as the first wing of a Commonwealth National Library. I loved the building and spent many weekend hours in its stacks and reading room. Next door was the Patent Office, an attractive Art Deco building that had also housed the city's first courthouse and still had two cells in the basement. At the foot of Mount Ainslie was the wonderful Australian War Memorial, and we played hockey on cold winter mornings on the hockey field at Manuka or on the large oval across Limestone Avenue in Reid. The young capital city was like a scattered library of excellent buildings on a wide open plain and we were lucky to grow up in an uncluttered country town. My early familiarity with a small but impressive number of works of architectural quality has made me think carefully before I insert a building anywhere in Canberra. Perhaps some of our politicians and business leaders might take the time to understand the spirit of the place before they trumpet silly ideas for the next building in the wrong place.

My interest in design and the making of buildings and public places comes also from time spent with our next-door neighbour John Scollay. John's elegant houses in Canberra's inner suburbs, with their low-pitched gable roofs, wide eaves and long unbroken rooflines, have been described as part of a post-war 'Melbourne regional style of architecture'. John was a gifted illustrator and watercolourist and I have two of his paintings of the southern tablelands landscape. Tony and I were influenced by his gentle and creative approach to architecture although, for a time at least, I imagine I was even more impressed by the music he played on his ever-present banjo. When he left school, Tony went to work for John and later became a partner with him and Theo Bischoff in the well-regarded architectural practice of Scollay Bischoff and Pegrum.

When John Scollay was appointed University Architect in 1953, he took us to see the work under way at University House and the John Curtin School of Medical Research, the first permanent buildings at the new Australian National University.

I was attracted then and thereafter to the idea of special buildings for new and exciting purposes. I was also interested in Denis Winston's planning and landscape designs for the campus and in the way that Brian Lewis brought art and craftsmanship into his designs for University House. The John Curtin School was of considerable local interest because it was the first building in the national capital city to cost a million pounds. The builder was Karl Schreiner, who successfully tendered for its construction with a price of £999 999. Occasional meetings on site with the somewhat eccentric Schreiner no doubt increased my fascination with architecture and building.

Karl Schreiner came to Canberra from Austria in 1949 and established himself as a builder with offices in Lonsdale Street in Braddon. He was noted for his concern for the welfare of his workforce, many of whom he brought out from his homeland. Schreiner drove a fine Austin Healey 3000 roadster and sponsored a Bavarian oompah band that turned up in lederhosen and the occasional dirndl at public gatherings all over town. Canberra architect Neil Renfree recalls one of Schreiner's newspaper advertisements that said he needed a carpenter who 'must also be able to play the euphonium'. Schreiner built workshops and recreation facilities for his staff on rural land by the Cotter Road, a site earlier used as a construction camp for the nearby water and sewerage treatment works. A large and attractive pond in the northern corner of the site was the focus of extensive landscaping works by Schreiner. Stormwater was harvested and piped into this pond for irrigation, making Schreiner one of the pioneers of urban environmental management in Canberra. In 1968, the Department of Defence was looking for accommodation for its newly established Joint Services Wing and the Weston Creek site was recommended as available for this purpose. A short but fascinating slice of Canberra's post-war development and of my earliest interest in architects and builders came to an end in 1999 when the Schreiner settlement was demolished to make way for the Australian Command and Staff College.

At the Leaving Certificate in 1955 I was awarded a Commonwealth Scholarship and a Canberra Scholarship but if I had accepted either I would still have had considerable difficulties meeting the costs of living away from home. The Australian National University had no course in architecture, and still doesn't. I considered studying in Melbourne but settled on the University of Sydney because it was closer. With the encouragement of my father, I took up a cadetship with the same Department of Works that had brought us from England eight years before. The deal was simple and fair; the Department would pay me every fortnight during my five years of study and I would work for them for five years after I graduated. I learned much later that the contract was actually not enforceable because I signed it when underage, but I would have completed the five years anyway and I was one of the first cadets to do this. I had an income now, so I could afford to stay on campus. I chose St Andrew's College because it was Presbyterian; I had gone to an Anglican church for all my years in Canberra and thought I deserved a change. I borrowed the money to buy a very secondhand blue Singer sports car named in fluorescent paint by one of its previous owners as 'Bernadine'. It looked as if it could make the long drive up the Razorback in good weather and Bernadine and I headed off for Sydney.

*Days of Wine and Roses*

I moved with my few belongings into St Andrew's College in February 1956 and stayed there for the next five years. I joined the University Hockey Club and played in the Sydney first grade competition and at inter-varsity carnivals in Sydney, Melbourne, Adelaide and Perth. I graduated in 1960 with the degree of Bachelor of Architecture and was awarded a University Blue in Hockey. An early highlight of my short sporting career occurred in my first year in Sydney, when the Pakistan Olympic team stopped by on their way to the Olympic Games in Melbourne and asked us if we would kindly play their hockey team in a warm-up match. We naturally agreed and turned out on the women's hockey field in clean shirts and sandshoes (studs were not allowed on the women's green). The player I was marking was the fastest man in Pakistan and their hurdles champion and when he got past me it was all over red rover.

**Back Row** (left to right): J. Ellem, Joe Rajaratnam, B. Hando, C. Sivanesen, M. Curtin, R. Pegrum, Jim Rajaratnam, B. Reid.

**Front Row** (left to right): K. Roby, K. Mayman (Captain), P. Le Messurier, B. Pryor (Vice-Captain), T. Cheah.

Pakistan beat us by 19 goals to 1 in front of a small but spirited crowd. In hindsight, it was not a bad result, at least we scored a goal. At the Games in Melbourne in November, only India, Germany and Great Britain scored against Pakistan, who lost to India for the gold medal by one goal to nil. At a dinner in the Great Hall in 2007 to mark the centenary of hockey at the University, much was made of the fact that we had brought home the Syme Cup at inter-varsity competitions in 1959 in Melbourne (and again in 1961 in Hobart, after I had left the University) but that no Sydney University team had done so since that time. Five survivors of those teams were in the Hall that evening; Ken Mayman (our captain and the scorer of the lone goal against Pakistan); Bruce Pryor (vice-captain with the dangerous job of stopping my push in at short corners and then getting his hand out of the way before Ken cracked the ball at the goal); Richie Barnard (an incredibly fast and hard to stop fellow who went on to play for New South Wales) and Victor Pannikote (our fearless goalkeeper in the days when you wore a mouthguard and a box but had very little other protection). We wondered then and wonder still how we did it.

In January 1957, I joined several hundred other eighteen-year-olds for National Service at the Ingleburn army base south-west of Sydney. The ninety day basic training was shrunk for university students to seventy-seven days and we missed only two weeks of the first term. I learned a lot of skills I hoped I would never need to use like stripping and cleaning a heavy .303 rifle, throwing grenades with a straight arm and bayonetting straw sacks while screaming like a banshee. A month after we started, in a mock war game known as silly buggers, I was shot at by a short-sighted engineering student and a piece of shrapnel stuck in the end of my nose. They drove me back to camp and washed and dressed my eyes and gave me an eye patch. My friends told me I looked like Errol Flynn. I went on to light duties in the kitchen for a week (someone said they put bromide into the mashed potatoes, but that was a Furphy). For the next three years I remained on the Army Reserve with the Sydney University Regiment and attended winter camps in the Hunter Valley. I think we were a disappointment to the officers because we didn't really take it very seriously, but I must say I rather enjoyed the long route marches and camping under the stars.

I used my dear little Bernadine at weekends to travel with teammates to hockey matches all over Sydney. Every few weeks I drove home to Canberra, taking my washing and returning well fed and with cakes and biscuits and fruit. Nowadays this is an easy drive on a multi-lane motorway but in the 1950s the steep hills of the Razorback Range from Camden to Picton tested many cars and drivers. I usually set out in the early evening, hampered a little by rather dim headlights and stopping every now and then while the engine cooled down. Once a year or so, I would break down and telephone my brother Tony, who always had smarter and more reliable cars, and he would bring a rope and tow me home. At the time I smoked a pipe, oh so cool, tapping it out as needed on the running board. One dark night, in light rain and with no moon, I left Mittagong behind and had been on a long straight stretch of road for some time when my pipe slipped out of my hand onto the road. I drove slowly back and forth a few times until I saw the pipe in the middle of the road. I picked it up but then could not remember which way I had been going. I wasted fifteen minutes driving back to Mittagong. Canberra drags you back but the distance stays the same.

It was common some years ago to play down the quality of architectural education at Sydney and elsewhere in the 1950s and 1960s. There was and is no easy way to compare teaching staff or facilities or curriculum content among schools of architecture, but I felt that our tuition was, for the most part, excellent. The list of lecturers and studio masters was to my young mind impressive. There was a rigorous program of classes in freehand and technical drawing and a range of rendering techniques including endless ink washes over classical compositions—not terribly useful in the office even then but it taught us to think with our hands and take care of our drawings.

One of our tutors was the Hungarian architect and cartoonist George Molnar, who had earlier worked in Canberra for Ken Oliphant. Molnar encouraged us to look at the way that architecture reflected the society that produced it, not a bad way really to look at Budapest or even Canberra, then or now. Patrician in bearing and always well dressed in a central European way, Molnar was a notoriously difficult person to please. His cartoons for the *Sydney Morning Herald* were elegant and sparse. Robert Hughes was a fellow student with a talent for dynamic pen and ink sketches and for whatever reason Molnar could not stand him. Hughes had been commissioned to illustrate Elizabeth O'Conner's book *Steak for Breakfast* for serialisation in the *Herald* and was one day working on a sketch in the studio when Molnar walked by. 'You will never be able to draw ... you know nothing about art', said Molnar. He was a bit off the mark there. Hughes gave up architecture soon afterwards and in 1970 became art critic for TIME magazine in New York, from where he was for some years perhaps the world's most influential authority on art.

I liked to wander through the design studios high up in the old sandstone quadrangle building and I thought the lecturers were firm but fair in their critiques of our work. Lloyd Rees and Roland Wakelin struggled to teach us watercolour techniques and the principles of composition. Professor H Ingham Ashworth smoked fat cigars and laboured over an illustrated history of architecture in the Middle East, which none of us had ever seen and which we thought he might not have seen much of either. Then, as now, students of architecture (and practising architects, too) needed guts to expose their work to the opinions of others. In my final year, our visiting critic was Robin Boyd, a leading light in Melbourne's progressive modern architectural scene. I had spent weeks designing a spectacular sports centre and Boyd gave me a hard time because my main arena was circular in plan. I told him it would be a wonderful setting for all sorts of games and events. 'You can't play tennis in a circle', said Boyd. I think I said he probably didn't like sport, which did not help much, but we both survived the encounter and so have hundreds of others before and since. Architecture is not always easy, but it's a struggle worth having. I do however remember thanking my friends at Bligh Voller Nield forty years later for building a circular tennis venue for the Sydney Olympic Games.

The late fifties did not appear at the time to be an especially fertile time for architecture in Australia. Robin Boyd's book *The Australian Ugliness* made it clear that we were running at full speed into a hell of featurism, views he developed further in his ABC Boyer Lectures under the title 'Artificial Australia'. But there were hints of some first-class work and the promise of an architectural renaissance in the near future. Harry Seidler's modernist house for his mother north of Sydney had won the 1951 Sulman Medal, the top award of the New South Wales Chapter of the Institute of Architects. Five years later, Arthur Baldwinson, a member of our faculty of architecture, won the Sulman Medal for the Hotel Belmont at Newcastle. The international competition for the Opera House on Bennelong Point was of course the high point of the period in Sydney. The New South Wales government wanted to announce that they would build the stunning design of Joern Utzon, but they were not prepared to publish his sketches, which did not sell his design at all well. This dilemma was solved when Baldwinson completed his painting of the future Opera House as viewed from the Harbour Bridge, a picture that propped up the hearts and minds of Sydneysiders through the long years of petty-minded disputes to come.

I was out of step then, and remain so still to some minds, over the political and professional brouhaha following the resignation of Utzon. We were all dismayed at his departure, regrettably a not-uncommon occurrence in the field of architecture, where politicians and accountants and lawyers are prone to blame the architect for a situation of their own making. At the time, leading architects from all over Australia joined students to protest and seek Utzon's return. When this did not bring back Utzon, anger and vitriol was directed at Peter Hall, the brilliant young Sydney architect who had been offered the poisoned chalice to complete the Opera House. Hall finished his work in 1973 but it would be another thirty years, and ten years after his death, before the Australian Institute of Architects recognised his remarkable achievements.

Students were introduced to the realities of building construction by Trevor Jones and I was taken with the notion that you can build almost anything you can imagine. I suspect that this interest in making things happen comes from my father. As he had told the Institution of Engineers in Canberra, the most remarkable thing about the Mulberry harbours was that anyone dared to build them at all. I found technical specifications, working drawings and architectural detailing quite absorbing, rather like writing or drawing in a secret code and absolutely necessary if you want someone to build the things you dream about and build them well. During University breaks, I came back to Canberra and worked in the Department, where there was an emphasis on architecture that related properly to its context and climate and on buildings that could be built without too much trouble (no curved walls please) and would not leak (box gutters *verboten*). The Department had a long commitment to Canberra and to architecture in all the States and Territories and had developed protocols for just about any possible construction challenge. The Department, like the offices of government architects and public works authorities in the state capital cities, was also renowned for the opportunities it gave to young architects and engineers.

My time in Canberra as a student architect and young graduate and later in private practice coincided with the first two terms of the National Capital Development Commission, which provided the Department of Works and architects and engineers all over Australia with opportunities such as had not been seen before and will never be seen again. The National Capital Development Commission had total control over planning, development and construction in the ACT from 1958 until the introduction of self-government in 1988. Regrettably, the Commonwealth Department of Works, with its skilled body of professional designers and engineers, was wound up at the same time, ending almost a century of service not just to the national capital city but to the nation as a whole.

At St Andrew's College, I enjoyed the support and friendship of the Rev Alan Dougan, the College Principal (known as 'the Bird') who was also an influential member of the Presbyterian Church in New South Wales. Dougan was for many years a judge for the Blake Prize, a national award for religious art, and he had a particular interest in architecture. In my third year, Dougan moved me to a tutor's room with its own bathroom, all the comforts of the world really. I became a mentor to younger students some of whom, like Bernard Au from Singapore, went on to distinguished careers in architecture. Bernard came to St Andrew's in 1957 as a student on the Colombo Plan, his passage by ship to Perth and then by crowded train across Australia coinciding with the arrival of thousands of Hungarians following the uprising in Budapest. I have enjoyed meeting up with Bernard in Singapore and Kuala Lumpur over the years and he has visited us in Canberra with his wife Anna. Bruce Pryor is another architect with whom I have been fortunate to stay in touch. We first met at Canberra High School, where his father taught science. In Sydney, Bruce was a student at Wesley College, practically next door to St Andrew's, and we played hockey together for all our time there. Bruce and his wife Jenny were in London at the same time as I was in the mid-sixties and he went on to become a partner in the busy Sydney office of Devine Erby Mazlin. Devoted to one another, Bruce and Jenny chose to take their lives together when he was diagnosed with motor neurone disease in 2017.

In 1959, St Andrew's College built a new refectory, one of the last buildings to be designed by Leslie Wilkinson, the foundation professor of architecture at Sydney University. I followed the work with great interest and spent as much time as possible with Wilkinson on site. Among other things, I learned the art of simple instructions to builders. One day, I heard the painter ask what colour blue Wilkinson wanted for a particular wall. Wilkinson, a heavy smoker, pulled out a packet of Craven A cigarettes and gave it to the man, saying 'match this'. At the request of the Bird and Wilkinson,

I painted the shields of the College, the University, the Church and New South Wales on the ceiling of the new dining hall, and these crests remain there still. The story of my original College crest is told in a plaque on the refectory wall. It seems that an almost identical version of the crest had been granted only a few years earlier to a college in Dunedin, New Zealand. Because Dunedin got theirs first, Andrew's had to make a few changes to my shield and the stars got jazzed up a bit.

My proud parents came to our graduation ceremony in the Great Hall in April 1961. I said farewell to St Andrew's and the University and headed back to Canberra where the Department put me to work full time as a base grade architect. It was time to see what the world was all about.

*St Andrews College Refectory*
*1960*
*Leslie Wilkinson architect*
Roger Pegrum

*Kings Avenue Bridge and the lake under construction 1963.*
*Left foreground is the Administrative Building (now John Gorton Building) by G Sydney Jones and Department of Works and Housing built 1947-1956; on Kings Avenue foreground centre is the first stage of the National Library by EH Henderson 1934 (demolished 1968); right foreground are the temporary buildings for Commonwealth government offices ('the woolsheds') which included the ACT regional office of the Department of Works.*
National Library of Australia

# The Swinging Sixties

*Six Years in the Sheds*

The Commonwealth Department of Works started its life as the Public Works Branch of the Department of Home Affairs, one of the seven Departments of State established in Melbourne at Federation. In 1916, the public works functions were transferred from Home Affairs to a new Department of Works and Railways. They were moved again in 1932 to the Department of the Interior and then in 1945 to a Department of Works and Housing. In due course this became the Department of Works and the head office moved from Melbourne to Canberra. With a few more name changes, and with regional offices in all the States and Territories, the Department maintained its role as the Commonwealth public works authority for over eighty years until it was abolished in 1988.

The development of Canberra as the seat of government had been slowed firstly by the World War and a general lack of enthusiasm to leave the comforts of Melbourne, and later by the Depression and a Second World War. When the Parliament moved to Canberra in 1927 with a skeleton public service, the administration of the city was in the unimaginative hands of the Department of the Interior, which ran Canberra as its own fiefdom, resenting its dependence on the Department of Works for construction and maintenance works. For the next twenty years or more, neither the government nor the bureaucracy showed much interest in turning Canberra into Australia's national capital city.

After the Second World War, moves to transfer public servants to the national capital were again resisted by powerful interests in Melbourne. Described a generation earlier as a 'handful of hovels in a howling wilderness', Canberra was in not much better shape when the Queen came to town in the summer of 1954. It was clear that Canberra would never be more than 'a good sheep station spoiled' without strong government support and a sustained injection of funds and goodwill. The government was told from many directions that it was time to fill in the gaps of the Griffin plan and make Canberra a capital city worthy of the nation. A Senate Select Committee was appointed to investigate the development of Canberra 'in relation to the original plan'. The Committee reported that the central areas of Canberra were like 'graveyards where departed spirits await a resurrection of national pride' and recommended there be 'a single authority for the development and administration of Canberra'. The government was stirred into action and Prime Minister Robert Menzies became Canberra's strongest supporter. 'Every nation needs a capital city', said Menzies, 'once I had converted myself to this faith, I became an apostle'.

The National Capital Development Commission (NCDC) was established in 1957 to 'carry out the planning, development and construction of the City of Canberra as the National Capital of the Commonwealth'. The NCDC was given control of all undeveloped land in the Australian Capital Territory with the condition that it 'not depart from, or do anything inconsistent with, the plan of the layout of the City of Canberra and its environs published in the *Gazette* on the nineteenth day of November one thousand nine hundred and twenty-five'. John (later Sir John) Overall, then Chief Architect in the head office of the Department of Works in Melbourne, was appointed as the first Commissioner of the NCDC supported by two associate commissioners, Grenfell Ruddock, also an architect, and Bill Andrews, an engineer. For the first ten years of its life, advice to the NCDC on all major development and planning proposals for Canberra was provided by a National Capital Planning Committee, which included Sir William Holford and representatives of Australia's professional institutes in architecture, engineering, town planning

*Walter Burley Griffin and Marion Mahoney Griffin at Castlecrag, circa 1930*

and landscape design. As an independent authority on architecture and town planning, Holford's influence as a member of the National Capital Planning Committee was considerable.

Not everybody welcomed the coming of the National Capital Development Commission and there was particular resistance from the Department of the Interior, which abruptly lost its control over planning and development in the Territory. Sir John Overall recalled in his memoirs that he had approached Bill McLaren, the Secretary of the Department of the Interior, for help in finding office space for the Commission and was told by McLaren to 'find your own bloody office'. Asked whether the Department of the Interior would work with the Commission on a particular project, McLaren is said to have told Overall 'pig's arse'. Thankfully, relations between the Commission and the Department of Works were a bit better than that. Operating on behalf of the NCDC, the Department was responsible for more than half of all construction activity in Canberra in the 1960s.

The Commission took over all eight floors of a nice new office building halfway up Northbourne Avenue and set to work on the design and construction of the central parklands and lake foreshores. Detailed planning in the national areas was hampered for a considerable time by uncertainty about where to put the permanent Parliament House. Griffin's plan had shown Parliament House on Camp Hill, a low rise below Capital Hill. In recognition of this, the provisional Parliament House had been built somewhat further to the north, leaving Camp Hill free for the permanent building sometime in the future. Holford said that the Camp Hill site was unattractive and too small, and that it was not reasonable to expect the present Parliament House to be demolished for some time. 'My own choice,' he suggested, 'would be in the centre of the (land) axis rather than at one end of it'.

For the next decade, work in the central national area, including critical decisions on the siting and detailed design of the High Court and the National Gallery, proceeded on the assumption that Parliament House would one day be built on the southern shore of the central lake. The NCDC said in 1967 that aesthetically speaking, the view is held by eminent authorities that the design of Canberra would be greatly enhanced by siting a major building at the central point of the Triangle ... a lakeside setting would permanently establish Parliament as the heart of the Government precinct ... there is no doubt that the permanent Houses of Parliament could be located on Capital Hill but there is every indication that locating them there would not have the convenience of the lakeside site.

Overall said later that trying to design the central areas of Canberra without a firm decision on the location of the Parliament House was like 'playing chess without knowing where the king was'. Holford's 'westminsterish' proposal lingered on until the mid-1970s, by which time the politicians had decided they would rather be on top of Capital Hill anyway.

The ACT regional office of the Department of Works was in a two-storey fibro building in Barton, part of a group of temporary government office blocks behind Kings Avenue known locally as the woolsheds. Vast drawing offices at the upper level for architects and engineers faced each other across large open gardens and there was excellent natural light from big windows. A heavy steel bundy machine was bolted to the wall at the top of the main staircase and we all had to clock in to work by 8.30 am and not leave before 4.51 pm. No coffee queues or flex-time in those days and no showers or lockers if you walked to work or rode a bike. We sat on high stools with double-elephant size drawing boards and long wooden T-squares and the older hands wore grey dustcoats or fabric sleeve protectors. At the far end of the drawing office were glazed cubicles for supervising architects and the principal architect and somewhere in there was the office of the ACT Director of Works. Otherwise it was just one big room, not broken up at all, the ultimate open office, oh, how the wheel turns. For more than thirty years, Canberra's sewer and stormwater drains, electricity networks, roads, schools, playgrounds, hospitals and houses were designed and documented in these humble sheds.

Near the middle of the drawing office sat Doug McCalman, a small man with a fine head of hair, up high on his stool with a cigarette always in the corner of his mouth, colouring perspective drawings with one hand and writing memorandums or specification notes with the other. Doug had transferred to Canberra from Melbourne in 1936 and for a short time before he went off to war had been the Chief Architect in the Department of the Interior. His talents were many and his stories fascinating and I was proud to sit and talk with him about things past, present and to come. Arthur Tow was a patient senior architect and a first-class designer who showed me dozens of ways to draw trees and taught me how to do aerial perspectives. My supervising architects were Noel Wright and David Ryan, to whom the most important attributes of a building were that it worked in plan, section and elevation.

The principal architect for the first part of my time back in Canberra was Bruce Litchfield, who had quite fixed ideas about what worked in buildings and what did not. He was particularly interested in windows—the only proper window, he said, is high to let in as much daylight as possible. It should slide up and down, which helps with natural ventilation, and the flyscreen must be on the outside because that is where the flies are and that is where they should stay. Livija Strauts was a wonderful draftswoman from Latvia who showed me how to look after my drawing instruments. The marvellous new Pelikan Graphos pens had just come on the market—we could all draw lines as fine as spiders' webs, but you had to know how to keep the nibs clean. I learned how to wash my setsquare with soapy water only, never methylated spirits, and how to prepare tracing linen with talcum powder. What excellent tutors I had.

I must have been missing the student life because by Easter I had enrolled in an arts course at The Australian National University with majors in English and German. It was a good time to study in Canberra. There were still tuition fees to pay but classes were small and lectures given during the day for full-time students were repeated after 5 o'clock for public servants. Imagine that today. I had outstanding lecturers like A D Hope in English and my German tutor was Dymphna Clark, the warm and wonderful polymath wife of Manning Clark. She told me grammar and declension were important but there was more to language than word endings and she wanted me to be able to recognise when I sounded right and when I didn't. I knew I was going to enjoy these courses. I graduated in 1968 without the conversational ease I had hoped for, but some years later I completed a program of the Goethe Institute which has allowed me to have reasonable discussions with friendly German speakers.

My first project as a graduate was a dog pound near the airport, all concrete and corrugated iron and chain wire and not much fun for me nor I imagine for the impounded dogs. I silently thanked Trevor Jones for his lectures on building construction which had removed the fear that I would draw something that no one could build. Then I was given a more interesting project, a visitor information centre at the Tidbinbilla Nature Reserve, which I modelled on a traditional timber homestead with generous verandahs on all sides. The building was soundly constructed and served well for many years but it burned to the ground in the bushfires of January 2003 and was replaced by something rather less attractive.

At the end of 1961, the NCDC commissioned the Department of Works to design and build the first school in Hughes, the entry suburb to Woden/Weston Creek, one of several new towns outside the Canberra valley designed to accommodate the expected growth of the city. The models for this dispersed development were the new towns set up in Britain after the Second World War. The British new towns

*Visitor Centre Tidbinbilla Nature Reserve 1962*
Department of Works

owed something to Ebenezer Howard and the earlier garden city movements but their principal aim was to prevent the uncontrolled expansion of London and major provincial cities to the north. Attracted by Holford's involvement with Canberra, town planners, architects, engineers and landscape architects from Britain and the Commonwealth who had worked on the British new towns flocked to Australia where they dominated the National Capital Development Commission for most of its thirty-year life.

*Provisional Parliament House, 1927. Government offices (West Block) behind.*
National Library of Australia

The older residential districts in the Canberra valley had been laid out somewhat romantically with tree-lined avenues and gracious crescents as part of Griffin's elegant geometry. These are Canberra's so-called 'garden suburbs', reinforcing in every way the landscape character of the city, valuable for their aesthetic returns as much as for their real estate worth. But post-war British town planning theory and practice was not about garden suburbs or attractive residential streets but more to do with traffic and land management and with organising citizens and communities for life in amorphous model suburbs, working in carefully grouped employment centres and driving about on efficient roadways. With only the merest of nods to the seemingly limitless Australian bush, the NCDC, acting on the strong advice of Holford, ensured that Canberra's growth would be accommodated in car-based suburbs in widely separated satellite towns. What I would describe later as a 'fanatical belief in the future of fossil fuels' turned the rolling hills of Canberra into an outback Los Angeles.

For more than a generation, and not always for the right reasons, Canberra attracted the attention of the world as an intensive laboratory for *fin de siècle* town planning and social engineering. We must however be grateful for the protections provided by the National Capital Development Commission which have spared the hills and ridges of the Canberra Valley from development. The NCDC noted that the National Capital Open Space System 'had its genesis in Griffin's sensitive perceptions of land forms and the importance of landscape and his reliance on them as the basis for his planning ... maintaining convenient access to the countryside, keeping clear demarcation between town and country by means of sharp urban edges and a keen respect for topography and landscape as important generators of urban form ... the mountain ranges that rise on the western side of the Murrumbidgee River and the lines of ridges and high hills to the east that contain and shape the urban expansion ... a wealth of natural and cultural heritage protected against urban development to serve the other long term needs of the National Capital. Such a resource is unparalleled in any other large city in Australia'.

Woden/Weston Creek had a design population of about 90 000 and plans showed a longitudinal town centre flanked east and west by residential districts varying in size at around 250 hectares. Each suburb would have a convenience shopping centre, a petrol station and medical centre or personal services building and one or more schools plus sites for scout halls and churches and kindergartens, all linked by a network of pedestrian and cycle paths. A neighbourhood 'home range' of about 400 metres placed every house within easy distance of schools or shops, a handy measuring stick but not necessarily a guarantee of a pleasant journey. Nor was there much logic to suburban subdivisions and it was easy to lose your way with no obvious road hierarchy or landscape framework and with streets and culs-de-sac looking pretty much the same wherever you went. Lovers of carefully laid out streets, footpaths and deciduous trees in the older parts of Canberra were also disappointed to find that seasonal variety and colour was mostly missing in these new communities.

Creative renewal of Canberra's new town centres in recent years has been hindered by rigid road reservations and the looming presence of internal shopping malls and large structured carparks. Dreams of medium density living with walkable streets and pleasant urban parks have been cast aside, at least for the time being, and housing choice in the town centres is presently focused on tower blocks. Consolidation and redevelopment in older and not-so-old suburbs has been equally disappointing. Mediocre residential outcomes have been practically guaranteed by tick-a-box planning policies and the absence of high quality design guidelines for streetscapes, landscapes and pedestrian amenity. In the NCDC era, innovative design briefs produced medium density housing at Swinger Hill and elsewhere which showed what could be done with cleverly planned courtyard houses on small plots of land in a tablelands climate. Michael Dysart's understated cooperative housing developments at Urambi in Kambah and later at Wybalena in Cook have deservedly become desirable addresses in otherwise predictable settings. It was perhaps inevitable that some of the more extreme NCDC planning experiments would not work out very well at all. Running local streets behind suburban cottages rather than in front of them, as pioneered with mixed success at Radburn in New Jersey USA, did no better in the suburbs of Sydney or Canberra because no attempt was made to design good-looking houses with more than one front door. Most unfortunate was an oversized public housing estate on the north side of town which was built in 1974 but demolished in 1991 when it fell into disrepair and vacant apartments were used by residents to stable horses.

*Hughes Primary and Infants' School boiler flue, 1962*
Roger Pegrum

Late in 1961, the Department appointed me as project architect for the primary and infants' school in Hughes. The general area was almost flat, and I suggested somewhat cheekily that the building needed something that stuck up in the air a bit so that people would remember where their children were during the day. With the benefit of hindsight, my thinking at the time was not much different from that of I M Pei when he arrived in Canberra from New York in 1980 to join the jury who would select a design for the new Parliament House on

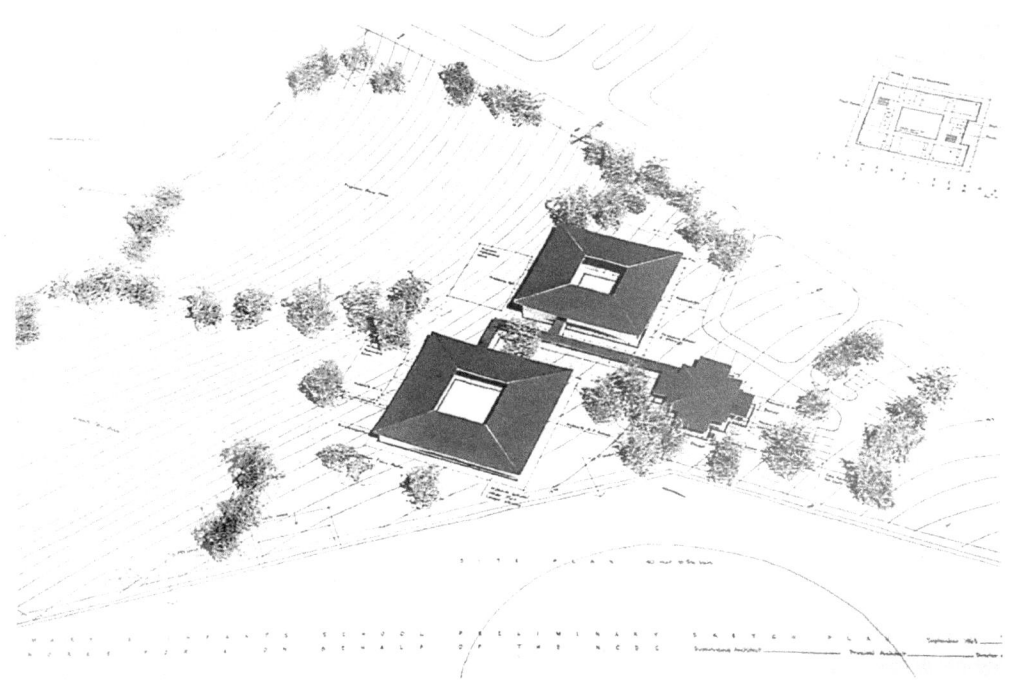

*Primary and Infants' School*
*Garran: model*
Roger Pegrum

*Primary and Infants' School*
*Garran 1964*
Roger Pegrum

Capital Hill. Asked by the local press if there was anything special he was looking for, Pei said he thought it would be a good idea if the design 'looked good on a tea towel'. I laid out the school with two long, thin, parallel classroom blocks running east-west linked by a triangular building containing the assembly hall, canteen and boiler house. I had some fun surrounding the lofty boiler flue with brickwork on a steel frame. The engineers at Works gave me my head and I was allowed to carry my ersatz campanile upwards well beyond what was needed for its function. I am not sure that the boiler flue ever made it onto a tea towel, but the strong and simple lines of the buildings looked good on aerial photos and early street maps and the equilateral triangle became the distinctive logo for the school. The school and the boiler flue remain in good condition.

The school at Hughes was opened in 1964 by the Minister for the Interior, Doug Anthony, whose children were pupils at the school and whose house was the first one you came across on the road into Woden. The school was well received and I was asked to design some more. It would not be possible, I was told, to have different designs for each and I had to come up with buildings suitable for a range of solar orientations and topography. I settled on a grouping of three nominally square buildings—a two-storey primary classroom block and a single-storey infants block, each built around a large internal garden, plus a free-standing building for the school auditorium, tuckshop and plant rooms. With different arrangements on site and with variations in materials, colours and rooflines, these schools popped up all over the place. The first one opened in 1967 in Garran not far from my own house and two of my children started kindergarten there in 1973. I took them out before the year was up when their teacher sent home a note asking me to please stop teaching them to read and write. It was my job, she said, to house and feed them but it was hers to educate them. Oh dear.

The Department of Works was not essentially risk-averse but we stuck with proven construction techniques and practised commonsense in both design and siting. The clay soil of Canberra has always been dangerously reactive, swelling after rains and shrinking in times of drought. Concrete footings for government buildings were therefore given heavier reinforcing top and bottom to resist uplift and cracking. Building orientation was critical for adequate natural lighting throughout the year and to take full advantage of Canberra's clear skies and average of more than seven hours of sunshine a day. We mastered the use of roof overhangs to cut out unwanted summer sun but to allow sun to enter in winter. Testament to the design and construction skills within the Department in the immediate post-war years can be found in the small number of extant public works and particularly in inner-city schools, of which the schools at Yarralumla and Turner and Harry Foskett's primary school in Hobart Avenue remain excellent examples after almost sixty years of service.

Twentieth-century controls over building design and construction had their worthy origins in movements to improve community health and personal safety. But in the nineteen fifties and sixties, there were no national regulations for the Australian building industry and standard codes of practice were in their infancy. The ACT Building Manual in 1960 said only that a habitable room must have a window or windows with an area not less than one-tenth of the floor area and that half of this must open for ventilation. A minimum ceiling height of 9 feet in habitable rooms was strictly enforced. Toilets had to be separated by an airlock from living and sleeping areas and have a window with a fixed fly-screened opening to the outside air. Toilet doors had to be fitted with spring devices to keep them shut so the pan was not on show when nobody was using it. You could have a kitchen opening to a bathroom but never to a toilet or a laundry. The dour and omnipotent Scotsman in the Department who oversaw plumbing and drainage throughout Canberra told us he would never allow anyone to 'mash potatoes with one hand and stir dirty nappies with the other'.

Standards for building materials were similarly straightforward. The performance standard for clay/shale bricks said little about structural strength or composition but was adamant that two bricks, when struck together, 'shall give a loud, clear ring'. It was assumed that houses would have external walls of cavity brickwork and pitched roofs with terracotta or sometimes concrete tiles. Profiled steel tray roofing had emerged as an economical alternative to tiles but was not yet available in long lengths, so that larger buildings usually had quite complicated roof plans. All this practical stuff gave me the best possible training and stood me in good stead when I went into practice on my own account a few years later. It was of interest also that, until at least the mid-1960s, the Commonwealth Bank and other retail banks made clear their preference for traditional materials and construction for suburban houses, applicants for mortgages being required to tick boxes such as 'roof—tiles or other' and 'walls—brick or other' with the implication that too many 'others' might damage your chances for a long-term loan.

The architecture curriculum at Sydney had included only passing references to the practice of architecture; there was hardly a mention of business planning, getting on with other consultants and builders or all the little, and not so little, challenges waiting for us in the future. In the Department, I had a vast drawing office full of people from all over the world and I learned something useful and often amusing there every day. From friends in other Canberra offices I also learned something of how it all worked in private practice. There were many stories about Ken Oliphant, Canberra's first resident architect. He was notoriously difficult to please on site but he knew when to concede defeat and could resolve most problems because he understood the limitations of both building materials and tradesmen. One story involved a large house in Tasmania Circle, where Oliphant had asked the bricklayer to build a sample panel for a fireplace. When Oliphant saw it, he said it was not good enough and please do it again. He did not approve a new panel on the next day and, when shown a third sample wall, is reported to have told the bricklayer 'if that's the best you can do, I had better accept it'.

Sometime in 1962, Canberra's population reached 70 000 and it became Australia's largest inland city. The town was on the move and the rest of the country was starting to show some interest in its young capital city. The Monaro Mall in Civic was Australia's first three-level shopping centre. Medium-rise office buildings were popping up on London Circuit and in Hobart Place and large construction companies like Civil and Civic had come to Canberra. There was a story, possibly apocryphal, about a busload of visiting school children who were driven around to see all these new buildings and when asked at the end of the day what Canberra's motto might be told the teacher that they thought it was 'Civil and Civic'.

I was kept in touch with what was happening at the NCDC through a number of school friends who were working there and by George Saldais, an architect who had graduated in my class at Sydney. John Dalgarno, also a cadet architect, left the Department of Works to join the busy practice of Kevin Curtin and Partners in Civic. It sounded like a fun office. John told me they had run a competition to see who could write the shortest building specification for a ski lodge they were designing. Departmental specifications for workmanship and building materials were always lengthy and highly detailed. I liked the winning specification from those at Kevin Curtin which fitted on a single page with one-liners like 'paint all things normally painted'. Another competition challenged them to write notes on their drawings in rhyme. I was much amused by a finely detailed drawing of a staircase with two lengthy arrows and instructions to the builder to 'install with care/ timber handrails here/and there'.

Away from our offices, we were a trendy little lot, meeting at Lumby's basement café in Civic after work for the new cappuccinos and Danish pastries. We polished our not very new cars for weekend drives into the countryside, the girls in brightly coloured knee-length frocks and the fellows in turtle necks and desert boots and, at that point, still with short hair. There were always cakes and goodies to be had from school friends now working in the kitchens at Parliament House and we carried scissors in the gloveboxes of our cars so we could cut flowers from the Senate gardens on the way to pick up our girlfriends. We sat around the swimming pool at the Canberra Rex Hotel and puffed away on Peter Stuyvesant cigarettes while people filmed us for cinema commercials. Television came to Canberra in 1962 when the *Canberra Times* and local radio station 2CA started broadcasting for a few hours each day from a large shed at the top of Black Mountain. The best shop for men's clothes was R T Whyte's in Kingston and I modelled clothes for them once a week live on television during breaks in the *Phil Silvers Show* and *I Love Lucy*. I drove my little car up Black Mountain at night and Whyte's paid me from time to time in spunky new clothes. I thought it was a good deal.

The Canberra community has a long history of involvement with music and the theatre. Canberra Repertory was established in 1932 and had staged a wide range of productions around town at various venues. In 1952, the 'Rep' was offered a permanent home in the old canteen building at the Riverside Hostel just behind our offices in Barton. Jim Birrell, later the author of the first book on the work of Walter Burley Griffin and later still a Gold Medallist of the Institute of Architects, was a cadet architect with the Department of Works at the time and he designed the sets for several Repertory productions. In his autobiography *A Life in Architecture*, Birrell recalls with some glee his production in the round of *The Philadelphia Story*, with a special opening night attended by the outgoing and incoming Governors-General Sir William McKell and Field Marshal Sir William Slim, during which his sets collapsed onto the front row vice-regal laps.

I had no previous experience in the theatre but I joined Repertory anyway and got a tiny part as a soldier in the world premiere of the musical *Boydtown* in the Riverside theatre, all about Twofold Bay and the Garden of Eden and whaling, not easy to do well on a stage not much bigger than a school bus. There was a brief step up to stardom with the Theatre Players in October 1962 when I played Tim in the musical *Salad Days*, which ran for seven nights at the Albert Hall to packed houses of family and friends. We got some nice reviews. C S Daley wrote in the *Canberra Times* that there was never a dull moment, citing Shakespeare's Cleopatra about all sorts of funny things happening in our salad days when we were 'green in judgment'. A review by Hope Hewitt in *The Bulletin* headed 'fresh, crisp and good for you' said that 'the central couple of Constance Vayne and Roger Pegrum were as handsome and agile a pair as anyone could wish'. I quit the stage while I was ahead after a short run of Noel Coward's *Hay Fever* in the theatrette at the Institute of Anatomy, in which I carried a tennis racquet all the time, nibbled at soggy toast and talked a load of rubbish for nearly two hours. I did not keep up with many of my fellow thespians but many years later at a barbecue in Bowral I ran into Ainsley Gotto, who had appeared in our production of *Salad Days*. In 1968, at the age of twenty-one, Ainsley became Prime Minister John Gorton's private secretary, the youngest person ever to be appointed to such a position. Thirty years on, we had a warm and pleasant chat about her stellar career and our brief brushes with fame in local theatrics.

In the middle of 1962, and quite out of the blue, the Principal Architect called me in to say that the National Capital Development Commission had asked if they could borrow me to assist Sir William Holford in the design of Anzac Parade. Construction of the central lakes was well under way at the time and the Kings Avenue Bridge was nearly complete. For the first time, it was possible to imagine the lake and see the full length of Griffin's land axis from Parliament House to Mount Ainslie. To the west of the Parade is Reid, one of Canberra's oldest residential precincts. We laid out sites for memorials along the Parade which picked up on the street pattern of Reid and we used the rhythm of central planter beds to define the gentle rise of the land and crushed red brick paving to bring a human scale to the long composition. We added a shallow chicane at the bottom end of the Parade, requiring not quite a genuflection but at least a sideways glance from drivers on Constitution Avenue, predictably lost not long after to the importunities of the traffic engineers.

*Anzac Parade model 1963 (with pipe and tobacco)*
Roger Pegrum

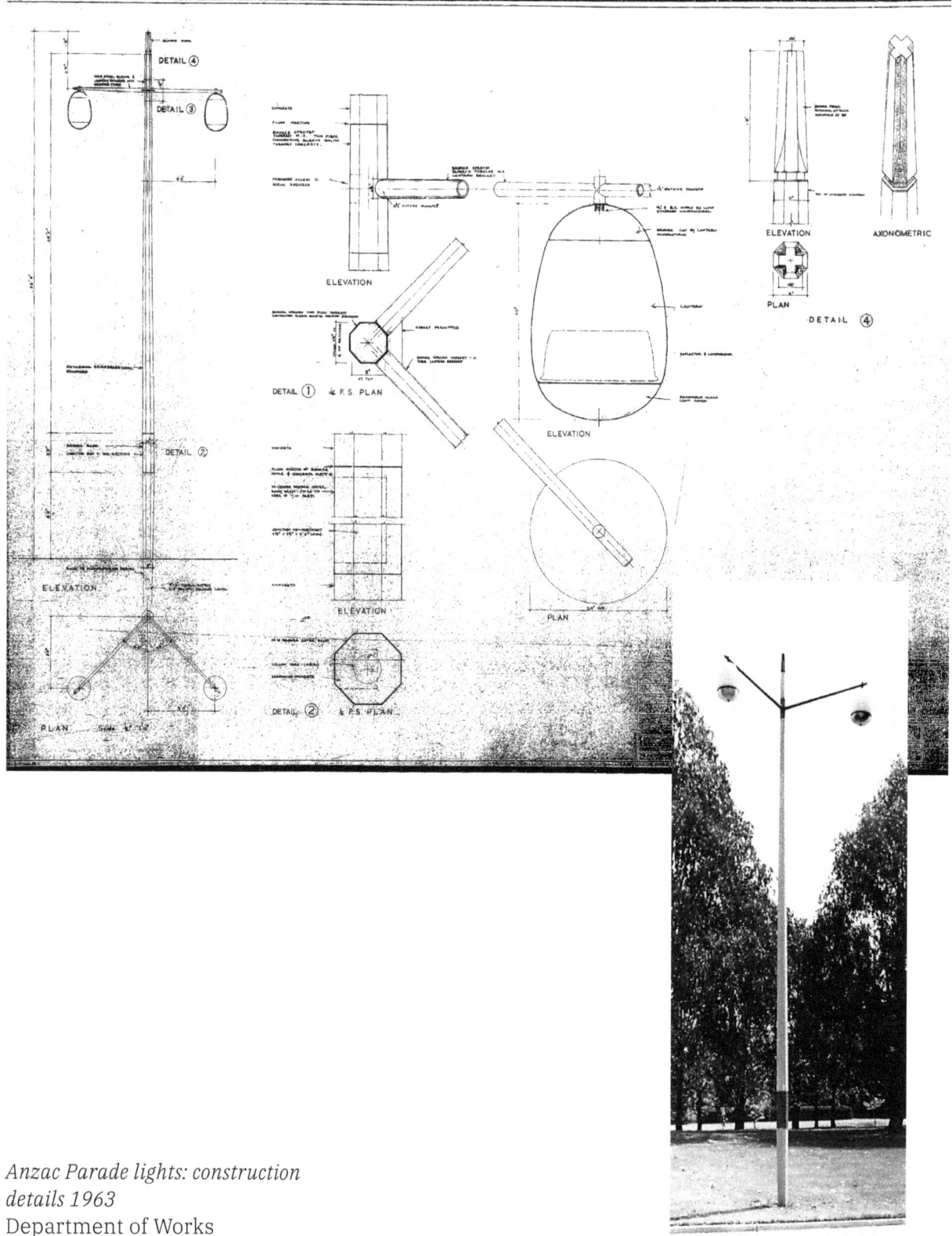

*Anzac Parade lights: construction details 1963*
Department of Works

*Anzac Parade completed 1965*
National Library of Australia

I worked in the NCDC offices for more than two months and I enjoyed the support and encouragement of Holford and his partner Richard Gray. 'What are you doing about lighting the roadway?' I asked them, 'it could be quite striking at night'. 'We thought you might have some ideas for us', they said. Everyone seemed relaxed about it all, but I was panicked. What did I know about streetlights? What could be good enough for what they were saying would be Australia's most sacred avenue, more recently described as Canberra's 'most considered street'?

I recalled a visit to Melbourne with the Sydney University hockey team only a few years before when I had admired the ornate streetlights on the bridge over the River Yarra at Flinders Street Station. The key features of these standards were (and still are) the oversized glass spheres each side of a short and fat central pillar. I played with designs for tall hexagonal poles with paired luminaires at the end of long outstretched arms, metaphors perhaps for the short but rich history of cooperation and collaboration between Australia and New Zealand, reaching out across the ditch as it were, firm and immutable, welcoming and embracing. I sketched large egg-shaped globes hanging from bronzed arms at right angles and finished the slender poles with a tall bronze finial. I made a neat little model using white painted acorns for the lights. When Holford asked me the scale of the model, I told him it was 'acorn scale' and he laughed out loud.

Holford and the NCDC loved the design and so did the Department of Works, where design development of the poles and lights received thoughtful and creative attention from our structural and electrical engineers. With Holford's endorsement, the Commission ordered more than fifty concrete poles and a hundred supersized white luminaires plus a shed full of spares. The giant Philips company made very large Edison screw incandescent globes and the 'eggs' were formed in translucent white fibreglass. The lights were switched on by Prime Minister Menzies on Anzac Day 1965, the 50th anniversary of the landing at Gallipoli. The lights became an integral part of the vista from the provisional Parliament House, listed on the then Register of the National Estate, where the lights and poles were recognised for their 'contribution to the design excellence of the place' and as a 'guard of honour' by day. I called the lights my 'Whitehall solution' and I was thrilled when Shibu Dutta referred to them as a 'string of pearls,' and when this became a common soubriquet. Thirty-five years later, the lights and poles had reached the end of their serviceable life and it was necessary to find a replacement design. The new poles and luminaires by Richard Johnson and Alex Tzannes are the successful result of a competition conducted by the National Capital Authority of which my wife, Annabelle Pegrum, was then chief executive. The design repeats my outstretched arms but with new energy-efficient light-emitting diodes by Barry Webb and maintains the night-time ribbon of lights when viewed across the lake.

Holford was pleased with my work and told me I should come to see him at their office in London if I ever went to England. The Department said I could go 'for a year or two, no longer' and I assured them I would be back. The Department registered me as an architect before I went away, which helped me get a reasonable salary in England. There weren't many architects on the Canberra register at that time and I was given the nice low number of 129. Today in the ACT only Enrico Taglietti on 14 has a lower number. I needed a passport too. It seemed like a good time for the Pegrum family to be naturalised as Australians and in November 1963 we all were given certificates of registration as Australian citizens.

*Travel is good for you*

A friend from school working in a travel agency in Civic booked my passage from Sydney on the maiden voyage of the *Guglielmo Marconi* in January 1964. It was just before the Boeing 707 took over from the passenger liners, and the elegant *Marconi* was packed with young Australians off to doss down in south-west London and take the grand tour of Europe. Primarily a tourist class ship, there were first-class staterooms on the boat deck for a small number of passengers, who included Marconi's granddaughter Elektra. My travel agent friend gave me a four-berth cabin all to myself with a small porthole. Leaving Melbourne, I was vomiting over the side of the ship into the Bass Strait when I met Robert Bruce from Orange, who was similarly indisposed. Robert was in a cabin near the Plimsoll line, full of heavy-drinking card players who had short tempers and sharp knives. I rescued him and he moved up to my cabin but we spent most of our time on the first-class lido deck with Elektra and her friends. We found our way to their much smarter public rooms by entering the chapel from the tourist class side and leaving through the first-class doors. We left the ship at Naples and went by train to Rome, Florence and Venice and on to London. No clean air act yet, the buildings were black with soot and London was cold, damp and depressing. The Holford office at London Bridge was bright and cheerful and I was welcomed most warmly but I gratefully accepted an invitation to work instead at their office in Canterbury on the new University of Kent.

Holford's Canterbury office was in an attractive three-storey terrace house in Dane John next door to the remains of a Norman castle and not far from the Cathedral. The University project was being delivered on a 'fast track' system new to me, which involved meeting with the builders at the King's Head pub at lunchtime, handing over drawings produced that morning and finding out what information they needed from us for the next day. I was working on the details of a lecture theatre which was emerging from the soggy site at an alarming rate and I developed a special affection for builders who knew what they were doing and asked questions with enough time for the answers. The King's Head was the pub of choice for the office most evenings and was also for a period of time the green room for members of a touring repertory company. After a fortnight of evenings in the pub, I had fallen madly in love with a very young Jane Asher. I was about to declare my eternal devotion when I discovered she already had a boyfriend called Paul McCartney.

My brother Tony told me he would come over in mid-year and I plotted a short tour for us through Scandinavia and Europe. I joined the Automobile Association, bought a nice little white Austin Mini, painted the headlamps yellow and stuck a big GB sticker on the boot lid. Camping gear and a small tent was costly, but I saved quite a lot by buying the previous year's models in bright blue and yellow. Tony arrived on the *Orcades* at Southampton and I proudly collected him in my smart little car. I'm not driving around Europe in that, he said, and I must say the car did look very small all of a sudden. Tony went up to London and came back with a 3.8 Mark II Jaguar in a nice dark silver colour with chrome wire wheels, leather seats and a Becker self-seek radio. I am sure we were the only Australians who did Europe that year in a Jaguar.

We took the ferry to Ostend in June and had two pleasant weeks touring Norway and Sweden (Oslo, the Viking Ship Museum; Stockholm, the 1923 City Hall by Ragnar Ostbergs). Inevitably, we were drawn to the rich variety of buildings and streets both old and new, but it was otherwise probably the same tour taken by most Australians and New Zealanders visiting the old world for the first time—castles and galleries, ruins and gardens, new foods, different beers, wines and cheeses, long fast drives on the *Autobahnen* and *Autostrade* and friendly encounters with the rest of the world in camping grounds. We spent a day in Pompeii and watched Frank Sedgman play tennis in Switzerland. We saw *Madame Butterfly* from cheap seats up high in the Teatro La Fenice in Venice, and we saw *Aida* on the world's biggest stage at the Baths of Caracalla in Rome, complete with elephants and camels and galloping horses, all beneath a full Italian summer moon. In Copenhagen, we visited the Tivoli Gardens and Grundtvigs Kirke, the remarkable neo-Gothic church by Jensen-Klimt built, we were told, by the same gang of bricklayers working nonstop for five years and laying more than five million yellow-grey bricks.

We went to the Rijksmuseum in Amsterdam and the Reeperbahn in Hamburg. In Berlin, we camped on the Wannsee and found bullet holes in our tent in the morning because people had tried to escape during the night from the DDR by swimming across the lake. We loved *Ku'Damm* and the *Gedaechtniskirche* and crossed into a gloomy East Berlin at Checkpoint Charlie, with its ominous warning *Sie verlassen jetzt den Amerikanischen Sektor* (You are now leaving the American sector), feeling out of place in the Jaguar among Trabants and Wartburgs on wide empty streets, all very scary stuff. I took far too many photographs with my new Pentax SLR, particularly interested in getting up close, lots of windows and doors and kerbstones and gravestones. Panoramas can remind you where you have been but to find out what things actually are you have to get close and touch them. It was a grand tour indeed.

Back in London, Tony and I took a small flat in Finborough Road Kensington, which sounds like a cute local street but was in fact a wide freeway for huge trucks from Europe headed for every part of the United Kingdom. We had to buy ear plugs, just so we could sleep. We got jobs nearby in Kensington High Street with Llewellyn-Smith and Waters, a long-established architectural practice with brewery connections. A dear old lady sat at the front desk with a big book for us to sign when we arrived in the morning. At 8.30 am, she ruled a thick line across the page and you got a ticking off for being late. As the year came to an end, we got used to going to work in the dark and coming back home in the dark. They gave us luncheon vouchers you could use in a pub but not to buy drinks and sadly the work in the office was not very exciting. I was sent down to Newhaven in Sussex to look at a site for a bottling plant for wine from France and drew up a smart looking shed that seemed to please them and was built in a matter of weeks. I worked without joy for some time on a vast housing project for the Greater London Council, leaving me convinced that social housing on a large scale is an irreducible paradox. At the other end of the office, Tony was designing a very pleasant pub on a small city edge block with a high ceiling and big windows opening to a garden. That's no good at all, the boss told him, this is England, all you are looking for is a low-ceilinged room out of the rain, nice and cosy with a fire going, hold the courtyard and the sunshine until you get back to Australia.

London was nevertheless a fun place to be in the mid-sixties. Stamford Bridge was within walking distance and I became a loyal supporter of Terry Venables and Chelsea FC, following them to away matches in the home counties and going to international matches at Wembley. We found the Mods more interesting than the Rockers and soaked up Mary Quant and Vidal Sassoon and the fashions of Carnaby Street and Knightsbridge. The Beatles and the Rolling Stones were big and there was a pirate radio station named Caroline on a ship somewhere in the North Sea, playing music you couldn't get on the BBC. There were premieres of *A Hard Day's Night*, the first Beatles film, and *Goldfinger*, the third James Bond film. Sean Connery's Aston Martin went on display at the Earl's Court Motor Show and we motored down to the British Grand Prix at Brands Hatch. It was a good time for the Aussies at Wimbledon. Roy Emerson beat Fred Stolle to win the men's singles and did it again the next year after we had left. Margaret Smith was beaten in the final in 1964 but won in 1965. We were pleased to hear of gold medals to

Betty Cuthbert and Dawn Fraser at the Tokyo Olympics in October. There was also a busy expatriate social life and we went to weddings of Aussies with local lads and lassies all over England, regularly hiring morning suits from Moss Bros in Regent Street. On my first visit, the fitter asked me 'On what side does Sir dress?' A bit of a cheek, I thought at the time, but useful of course if you like comfortable trousers.

Through Robert Bruce, I met Frances Eisenman in London. Frances' father was American and she had been born in Hollywood but her mother lived in Dorset and was a leading breeder of Pekinese dogs and a judge at Crufts. Frances and I fell in love and were married at Wimborne Minster in May 1965. We flew to Australia via Jamaica and Mexico and found that Canberra was booming. The population had doubled in ten years and would double again in the next ten years. We rented a house in leafy O'Connor and bought a black retriever named Sophie and a pale green Mini Minor which we decorated with big white daisies. Frances brought Carnaby Street to Canberra when she started *The Clothes Line*, designing and selling the miniskirts and jumpsuits that were all the rage in London. At the Melbourne Cup the year before, public reaction to Jean Shrimpton's miniskirt had caused the young English model to say that perhaps Melbourne was not yet ready for her. But Canberra was certainly ready and gobbled up Sassoon and Quant and all that went with the Sloane Rangers. *The Clothes Line* was for two years a booming home business with outsourced seamstresses all over town and oversize printed labels on recycled cardboard. There were regular fashion parades and wine tastings at our house in what the *Canberra Times* insisted was 'Upper O'Connor', bits of fun in the fondue years when we all had parties to bottle wines brought from Mudgee in cardboard casks.

I went back to work in the Barton offices and for a short time in the new Sirius building in the Woden Town Centre. I had decided that I wanted to open my own architectural practice as soon as possible, and I took on a small number of private renovation jobs and toyed with a few schemes for speculative and project housing that came to nothing. My first significant private commission was for the Ryan house in Campbell, a modest two-storey design on the slopes of Mount Ainslie behind the War Memorial. My client was a young structural engineer who said he would like to use his skills in steel design and fabrication and I gave him a house with a simple steel frame wrapped in concrete bricks. Next door and using the same bricks is the Richard Barnard house designed by my brother Tony and our clients agreed that the houses sat well together in the street. Not long after, I built a second house nearby in Cobby Street on an irregular and sloping site with some interesting internal spaces around a trapezoidal courtyard. But it became clear that I could not expect to build a business as an architect while I was at the Department of Works during the day and sitting at a drawing board in the kitchen at night. My five-year cadetship with the Commonwealth was coming to an end and I decided to start in private practice once I had built our own house.

My parents helped us to buy a block of land in Garran, not far from the primary school I had designed before leaving for England. In those days, residential land was sold by public auction on a ninety-nine-year lease and there was no reserve price. Plans and surveys were supplied for the blocks on sale with good information about soil types and levels. I settled on an odd-shaped site at the end of a cul-de-sac because it had a great big rock shelf on the surface and this was clearly visible in the middle of the block. I thought the rock shelf might put off other bidders, which proved to be the case because I got the land for a very reasonable price. The auction at the Albert Hall in January 1966 was the last one before Australia went metric, so there was the unusual experience of signing a contract and paying a deposit in pounds and shillings and settling four weeks later in the new dollars and cents. I designed a flat–roofed house balanced on the rock, making sure all the drains ran outside the rock. A small glazed patio punched into the floor plan brought in light and winter sun throughout the day, all very welcome in a house with only one small oil-fired furnace in the main living area. The ability to see through and across the house made it feel bigger than it was, a layered effect I have used in many other buildings. I drove to Goulburn one weekend and bought a brick wall in an old warehouse about to be demolished. The bricks were soft pink sandstock laid in lime mortar. I had the bricks trucked to Canberra and paid the local boy scout troop to clean and stack the bricks around the block.

I was lucky to get Martin Huber as builder. Martin had built several houses for local architects and I learned a great deal about the art of building over the next several months. I took the opportunity with my own house to try out a few different things like taking the load of the roof on the external skin of brickwork rather than the inside wall. I had waxed brick floors in the kitchen and bright red and green wall tiles behind the benches and the cooktop. Electric cooktops and wall ovens were the latest thing, and I had read somewhere that you should prepare food under green light and cook it under red light. Internal walls were bagged and painted white with smooth set plaster in the bathroom. The toilet was in the bathroom, which was pretty daring in those days, and I put handbasins in the bedrooms, useful for changing nappies or cleaning your teeth or whatever. There was also a small projection room for home movies. The world premiere of Michael Edols' remarkable film *Titikawa and Friends* took place in our house where it was reviewed for the *Canberra Times* by Dougal Macdonald. The house created quite a stir when it was finished and it was a popular inclusion in the spring and autumn house tours organised to raise funds for local charities. A neighbour in the street was Ian Mathews, at that time editor of the *Canberra Times*. Ian asked me whether I would write articles on architecture and design from time to time and thus began an interesting second string to my life.

Our daughter Emma was born in Canberra in March 1967 and our second daughter Isobel in December 1968. We joined a British-Australian reunion association to take advantage of Qantas charter flights to England at reduced prices and Frances made plans to fly with the two girls to see her mother and family. When they left in the middle of 1970, Frances was pregnant and had provided Qantas with documentation showing that the baby was due in November or December. I stayed behind to work. Our son Adam was born in Bournemouth at the end of November and I joined them in time for Christmas. When we all turned up at Gatwick on 26 January 1971 for the long flight back, I was told I had to buy a ticket for Adam (who was not at all well and cried all the way home, which did not help things). No ticket, no flight, they said. But you flew him over here without a ticket and inside his mother, I said, it's Australia Day, fair crack of the whip. They won, of course, and I paid under duress but there was some interesting correspondence in the next few months with Qantas.

By the late 1960s, Canberra was no longer a small town. Social and political change was all around. The pop culture and protest movements of the sixties reached Canberra just in time for the seventies. New arrivals in town included several young journalists with whom I would be close friends for many years. Henry Plociennik and Chris Freeman had worked together at the Sydney *Daily Mirror* before moving to Canberra in early 1967. Henry later worked for the *Australian* and started a newsletter, *Skiing News*, for which I wrote articles about development at Falls Creek and Perisher. He returned to Sydney in 1970 with the *Australian* as senior reporter and occasional chief of staff and co-wrote a book on rock singer Johnny O'Keefe. Henry taught me a lot about how to write so that your reader keeps on reading. During the 1980s, Henry was the editor of *Woman's Day,* where he increased the circulation to more than 560 000. I saw more of Henry after I moved to Sydney in 1974 and he played a key role in the publication of *The Bush Capital* in 1983. Henry died of pancreatic cancer in 1989, a sad loss to the worlds of journalism and publishing.

Chris Freeman had been sent to Canberra with Henry to cover one or two sessions of Parliament as part of their training. They reported also on local demonstrations against the Vietnam War and South Africa's apartheid policies which had interrupted the relatively peaceful relationship between students, the police and the Canberra community. Chris joined the public affairs section of the Department of Immigration and later the Australian Government Overseas Information Service, responsible for projecting an accurate and contemporary image of Australia. I visited Chris when he was public affairs officer at Australian diplomatic missions in Kuala Lumpur and San Francisco and I stayed with him and his wife Janet twice when he was Australia's High Commissioner to Malta. Chris has been a loyal friend and confidant in many parts of my life and I value his friendship greatly.

Michael de Kretser was born in Ceylon, now Sri Lanka. He came to Melbourne as a teenager and was a student at Camberwell Grammar School, moving to Canberra in 1966 as a journalist with the *Age*. He played cricket for Singapore and could beat me easily at tennis and golf. When we moved into our house in Garran, the two of us played badminton obsessively in the back garden. I was best man at his wedding at Hanging Rock before he moved to Singapore, where he became a public relations superstar, famous among other outrageous promotions for persuading Madame Tussauds in London to stand a real Singapore Airlines 'Singapore Girl' in their wax museum. We saw each other here or there whenever we could, and I enjoyed his company and love of life for many years. On my seventieth birthday, Michael took me to Tioman Island in Johore, the Malaysian State in which I had been born. Michael died unexpectedly in 2017 as we were about to attend a function in his honour at Camberwell Grammar.

Back at the Department of Works I was put in charge of a number of projects at the provisional Parliament House. The Department was responsible for the almost constant rearrangement of functions and spaces within the House and the nearby East and West Blocks. I worked on various projects in the offices of the Prime Minister and the Cabinet, learning a good deal about the construction and detail of the original building and its several later additions. In 1967, Gough Whitlam became Leader of the Opposition on the retirement of Arthur Calwell. Whitlam inherited a run-down suite of offices, cobbled together from smaller rooms and enclosed verandahs with floor and ceiling levels all over the place. None of the chairs or desks matched, every filing cabinet was a different size and colour and I was told there was no money for new cabinets (those were the days). It was a satisfying refurbishment process. Labor Party rules required secret ballots of the caucus, so I fixed hinged timber panels to the walls which opened to form voting booths and could be folded away afterwards. With the cooperation of Whitlam's staff, we carried out a carefully-timed logistical exercise over one weekend when he was out of town, laying out the contents of the filing cabinets in tidy piles in nearby rooms on a Thursday afternoon and taking the empty cabinets out to Fyshwick where they were patched up and sprayed a lovely 1954 Pontiac Blue. The carpets were cleaned and everything was returned on Tuesday and put in place, with smart new desks and upholstered chairs and curtains. We got a nice thank you note from Whitlam for sorting that out. I also fitted out the office of the Secretary of the Department of Trade,

Sir Alan Westerman (his son John had been at Canberra High with me) in the Administrative Building. I built in a nice piece of joinery with a concealed refrigerator (rather more unusual then than now) in Australian timbers but forgot to allow sufficient ventilation so the refrigerator blew up. I got a minor ticking off, but the Department shielded me from anything worse.

For its whole life, the provisional Parliament House had presented an awkward and unwelcoming main entrance on Queen Victoria Terrace, with far too many steps up from the roadway, no handrails or balustrades to hold on to and no protection from the rain. Photographs and movie films from the opening of the Parliament by the Duke of York in 1927 show Dame Nellie Melba singing the national anthem under a decorative but temporary canvas awning. It had at last been agreed to give the front door a permanent canopy

and handrails and I was instructed to design these with minimum impact on the building itself. When Old Parliament House was placed on the National Heritage List in 2006, the statement of significance noted that 'the front façade of Old Parliament House including its entrance portico ... has been the setting of countless events, gatherings, protests and demonstrations (including) the dismissal of the Whitlam Government in 1975'. The (then comparatively new) canopy features in photographic records of events on 11 November 1975, when Gough Whitlam stood at the entrance to Parliament House and told the nation that 'nothing will save the Governor-General'. My modest entrance portico and handrails would seem to be well protected by one of the defining moments of Australian political history.

The Department of Works had given me opportunities I could have only dreamed about ten years earlier and I would leave my colleagues with some regret. The Department had served Canberra well through the first term of the National Capital Development Commission, which had been marked by both political stability and a confident national and local economy. The retirement of Sir Robert Menzies in 1965 led to Australia having three Prime Ministers in seven years. No longer the Prime Minister's favoured son, Canberra nevertheless continued to prosper. Talented young architects like Theo Hirsch joined the ACT office of the Department after leaving university and established designers such as Peter Staughton and James Maccormick were attracted to Canberra by the quality of work on offer. When Maccormick was appointed as Principal Architect in the ACT regional office in 1966, it was said that he was possibly the best-known architect Works had ever had. Both Staughton and Maccormick had spent time in the Melbourne office of Grounds, Romberg and Boyd and their designs showed the confidence and strong simplicity of form typical of that practice. Staughton's striking designs for the National Mint at Deakin did not proceed but the 'commanding presence' of his primary school in Red Hill was recognised fifty years later with the ACT Chapter Award for Enduring Architecture.

The Canberra office also assembled impressive teams of architects and engineers to design pavilions and exhibitions for international expositions in Japan and North America.

*Gough Whitlam's office*
*Parliament House Canberra*
*1967*
Department of Works

*Temporary canopy at opening of the Provisional Parliament House by the Duke and Duchess of York*
*9 May 1927*
National Archives of Australia

*Gough Whitlam speaking on the steps of Old Parliament House*
*11 November 1975*
National Library of Australia

The Australian pavilions at Montreal in 1967 and Osaka in 1970 were designed in the ACT office by Maccormick assisted by George Saldais, Theo Hirsch and Max Barham. The 1974 Australian pavilion at Spokane USA was designed by Richard Johnson when he was Principal Architect in the ACT regional office. Working in association with Maccormick, Johnson also designed the Australian pavilions for Okinawa in 1975 and Tsukuba in 1985. These were heady times for everyone, models and drawings all over the place with architects and engineers working through the night on remarkable projects for Canberra and for exciting foreign locations.

Architectural thinking in Australia at the time favoured dynamic structural systems, often heroic in their form. As a cultural barometer for the rest of the country, Canberra collected more than its share of these bold and fractured concepts. The National Capital Development Commission proposed to build large new office complexes for the expansion of existing departments and for major public service agencies yet to move from Melbourne. Harry Seidler and John Andrews were engaged for new buildings in Barton, Belconnen and Woden, and the Department of Works was briefed in September 1967 for new offices for the Department of Defence on a site to the northeast of Fairbairn Avenue. The scale of these buildings was new to Australia and coincided with an international architectural movement based on democratic order and responsibility. For the next decade, public architecture would be expressed in powerful images using strong geometric forms. This 'new brutalism' would turn up in all State capitals but its clearest expression could be found in 1970s Canberra with the National Gallery and High Court by Col Madigan and Christopher Kringas. Concrete in large areas can be depressing in inner-city environments, but in the clear skies of Canberra it made for a lively architecture. The move of the public service and national institutions to Canberra and the transformation of the city from its outback beginnings into the setting for dramatic political, social and environmental change formed an absorbing backdrop to my entry into the challenging world of private architectural practice.

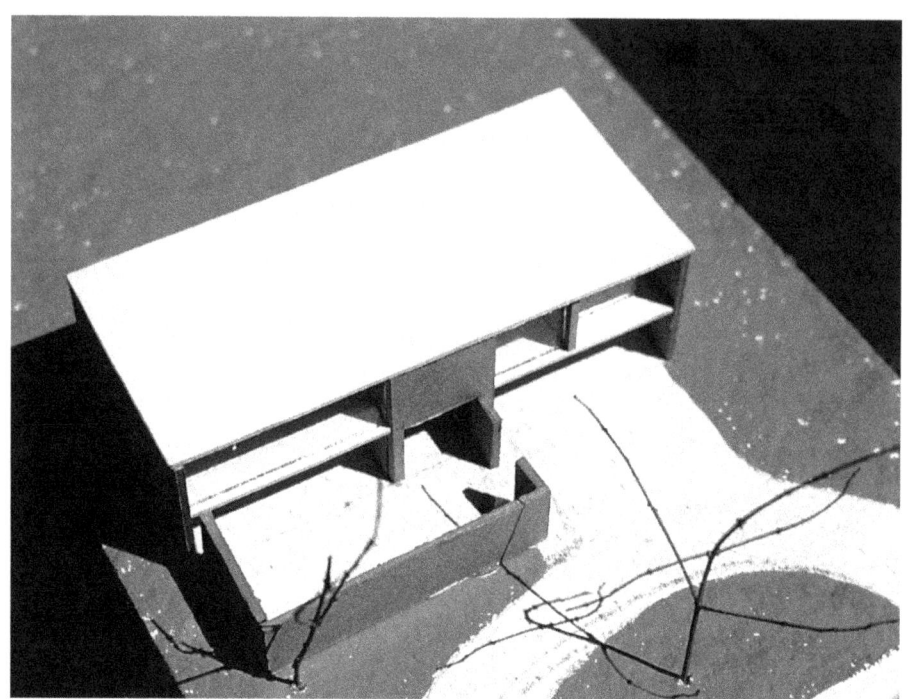

*Ryan house Campbell model 1967*
Roger Pegrum

*Stone Place Garran*
Roger Pegrum

# Private Practice 1

*The Early Houses*

We moved into our new house at Stone Place, Garran, in March 1968. When I opened my office in the city two weeks later, I had only one commission, a house in Aranda for Stephen and Ursula Conan-Davies. As was the practice then, I placed a small notice in Saturday's *Canberra Times* announcing I was open for business. One of my few telephone calls in the next week was from Gordon Shannon, a long and lanky chap who had been a few years ahead of me at Canberra High School and whom I knew also from our hockey playing days. Gordon had a senior position at the National Capital Development Commission and he was aware of my earlier work at the Commission with Holford on the design of Anzac Parade. Come and see me some time, he said. Over the next few years, the Commission offered me a range of work including design studies for residential subdivisions and local centres in the Tuggeranong Valley and the design of police guard boxes for foreign embassies. Together with a steady flow of private and project houses and commissions from the Department of Works, I had a pleasing variety of work over a considerable period of time.

I took space in the Center Cinema building in Civic, an innovative mixed-use building designed by Enrico Taglietti, with deep Vierendeel trusses at the ground floor level spanning over a large underground cinema. For the first few weeks, I shared two small offices at the back of the building with a start-up credit union but then Taglietti moved out and I took over his sunny rooms on Bunda Street.

My brother Tony, who by then was a partner with John Scollay and Theo Bischoff, told me in June they had decided to close down their office and we agreed to join together in a new partnership. Scollay, Bischoff and Pegrum worked at the time from one of the lovely townhouses in Arthur Circle designed by Roy Grounds after he had built the Academy of Science. Their office had a well-deserved reputation for its work and Tony had enjoyed excellent training and opportunities in all aspects of architectural practice. Tony had also worked for lengthy periods in Melbourne with Grounds and with the gifted structural engineer Norman Mussen.

The Canberra architectural community in the 1960s was small but was well supported in the residential sector by leaders in academic and business fields and by officers at all levels of government and the public service. We designed a house for a man who was about to be posted to Washington DC, had the house and garden built while he was away and then rented it out for him until he came home. Some of the bigger houses inevitably went to out of town architects and I enjoyed seeing how they responded to our site and climate. Ken Woolley did a splendid house on the side of a hill in the Woden Valley for Peter Samuel from the *Bulletin* and this impressed me greatly, but I was not so enthusiastic about a house in Aranda by Robin Boyd, which to my mind missed the whole point of being in a bush setting in the cool climate tablelands.

I was fortunate to have excellent staff over the next few years and it was a happy and creative office. I impressed on everyone that we needed to like our residential clients a lot because we would be working with them for a long time. They might forget the name of the builder, I told them, but they would not forget their architect, and not only if their house leaked or moved around. When a new client came to us for a house, I always asked one or more of my staff to sit in at the first interview. Later we would talk about whether they were nice enough to work with. We said no to a few folks this way but we probably also avoided some messy moments down the track. The clients we did take on set out on their adventure with enthusiasm and discovered that having a house built just for you and your family by dedicated tradesmen is one of life's great journeys.

Peter Swalling joined me from the Department of Works. Peter was and is an architect with a fine eye for design, and he prepared many elegant drawings before moving with his wife Jocelyn to Adelaide. Finn Stensrud, Liisa Helasjarvi and George Dolnik were first class draftsmen and they produced most of the working drawings for our projects. In the days when everything was in ink on tracing paper or sometimes linen, they approached their drawings as if they were finished pages in a large illustrated storybook. Each sheet was a careful composition, easy to read and understand and a pleasure to look at. They could all draw like angels and I still have many of the plans they prepared.

I was equally fortunate with consultants and builders. I came across Murray Northrop almost by accident early in my days in practice. Murray is a structural engineer who came to Canberra to supervise construction of the Reserve Bank building on London Circuit designed by Perth architects Howlett and Bailey. He decided to stay in Canberra and went into business with Bill Gordon. Murray gave me the best possible advice and support for many years. He seemed naturally to understand what I was trying to do with a building and he effortlessly built in the necessary common sense and steel to stop it sagging or falling apart. My favourite builder was Hubert Roetzer, who built eight houses for me over the next few years and I was grateful for the skills of other local builders including John Pfeiffer, Mario Binutti, John Anderson and John Ainscough, for whom I designed the successful range of Manor Homes.

My houses used a limited palette of external and internal materials. Walls were often bagged brickwork painted off-white but I also used pressed bricks from Bowral laid as facework and with soft joints struck flush. Windows were framed in western red cedar, with big sliding doors to the outside. All the architects in town were using the new awning sashes and hook hinges designed for Stegbar by Robin Boyd. Mission Brown was the colour of the popular timber stain at the time, but I made up a much darker mix, almost black. My roofs were flat and heavily insulated with concealed gutters or were quite steep with dark terracotta or concrete tiles. Houses on sloping sites often had split level plans and I avoided corridors wherever possible.

Internal walls and ceilings were usually off-white, with floors of polished timber boarding or unglazed quarry tiles and sometimes cork. I used some strong colours in kitchens and I liked glass mosaic tiles and timber bench tops.

Everyone, it seemed, wanted lots of storage space under the house for bicycles, snow skis and camping gear. The new suburbs of Canberra were riddled with Kombi vans, caravans and trailers. Large and small families asked for workshops and saunas or waterproof sheds for model railways. A house was not a home without a big fireplace, which the family also cooked on, and I built in swinging arms for big black pots of winter soups. Houses had one or more oil heaters but there was no such thing as central heating or sealed double glazing and air conditioning was unheard of. Special requests made each place different and stopped me from repeating myself. I designed a house in Cook for a couple with a fear of fire. I built their wall oven into a concrete surround and made sure there was always at least one shiny red fire extinguisher and a fire blanket in sight wherever they were in the house. One of my last houses in Canberra, and the last house built for me by Hubert Roetzer, was for Chris and Robyn Diener in the suburb of Melba. The Dieners have a long-term interest in Japanese art and design and we set out the house carefully with high ceilings and an exposed frame of timber posts and beams stained black. A calm and elegant house full of artworks and delicate joinery, it is in fine condition forty years later.

*Manor Homes 1970 -*

multi manor 1

manor house 1

*McCawley and Davidson houses Garran 1967*
*Scollay Bischoff and Pegrum:*
*Tony Pegrum*
*CS Daley Medal 1969*
*25-Year Award for Enduring Architecture 2008*
*Byam Wight*

For the next few years Tony and I had a steady flow of younger and older people who wanted to live in quiet surroundings a few minutes out of the city centre. Ken Woolley's project houses for Pettit and Sevitt in the northern outskirts of Sydney popped up in Canberra as attractive alternatives to the rather heavy-handed European garage-under houses on offer from speculative builders. I was approached to design a range of upmarket project houses for a local builder who wanted to compete with Pettit and Sevitt. I came up with the rather pretentious name 'Manor Homes' and started off with four exhibition houses side by side in the Woden Valley suburb of Mawson. The smallest house was a modest split-level we called the Multi-Manor and the biggest was of course the Manor House. In between was the Country Manor with wide verandahs and there was

*Chancery for Embassy of Japan 1971*
*Yarralumla ACT*
(in association with Japan Department of Works)

CHANCELLERY FOR THE EMBASSY OF JAPAN

an open-planned Mod Manor. I was surprised and delighted when these designs took off and turned up in all parts of town. Back in Canberra fifteen years later, I found that Harvey Jacka, my last departmental secretary, was living happily in one of my Manor Houses in Weston Creek.

In 1969, a year after joining me in practice, Tony received the CS Daley Medal for two modernist houses he had built side by side on the edge of the Federal Golf Course. One of the pair was only a few years later defaced by a local architect who should have known better but the other house at Furphy Place has been meticulously maintained by its original owner Margaret McCawley. In 2008, the McCawley house received the RAIA 25-Year Award for Enduring Architecture and in the same year was entered into the ACT Heritage Register. There was a minor legal skirmish when we discovered that Tony's plans had been copied and mirror-reversed for a house built in the adjoining suburb of Mawson. The drawings had two incorrect dimensions and a spelling error, each of which had been faithfully transferred to the pirated plans. Our actions for theft and breach of copyright got as far as the steps of the ACT Courthouse, at which point the guilty party (a senior member of the defence department who also should have known better) agreed to pay handsome damages. It is difficult enough sometimes for an architect to get paid but to win a legal battle and be paid twice was special indeed.

*The Eclipse competition
Circular Quay Sydney 1988*
Hassell Architects
with Ove Arup
Tony Pegrum,
Tony Dibden

Tony and I agreed our practice would work best if we presented ourselves as somewhat separate and so we called the office Roger Pegrum Anthony Pegrum Architects. We kept our own clients for residential work but stepped in whenever needed to look after the other's projects. Tony designed a number of houses in Woden, Belconnen and outside the ACT in Yass and in Jindabyne, but he was more attracted to commercial projects. It was an unusual but successful association. An article in the *Australian Home Journal* in April 1972 headed 'The Brothers Pegrum' rather embarrassingly wrote of the 'incredible success story of the thirty-three-year-old twins'. The freedom for us to work independently had significant business benefits. Early in 1970, I was approached by the Phoenix Assurance Group from Sydney to act as their project manager during the construction of their new Canberra office on Northbourne Avenue. The developer, no doubt keen to establish a good relationship with our office on the Phoenix project, almost immediately offered us a role as the Australian arm of the Japanese Department of Public Works in the design, documentation and approval of a new Chancery building for the Japanese Embassy on Adelaide Avenue. This suited us fine; I ran the Phoenix job and Tony spent much of his time for several months with Mr Sakamaki from Osaka.

Tony was a wonderful draftsman and he turned Sakamaki's rather disappointing sketches into a most beautiful set of construction details. Tony left Canberra in 1972 and moved with his family to Adelaide, the home town of his wife Geraldine. There he joined the office of Hassell McConnell, who had just completed the striking Festival Theatre on North Terrace. He became a partner at Hassell in 1975 and opened their office in Sydney, where he worked on major shopping centres and a number of city centre projects in New Zealand and south-east Asia. Tony retired in 1998 and died of a heart attack in December 2001. He had earned a national reputation in the fields of commercial and industrial design. One of his unrealised concepts was an elliptical office tower for the challenging eastern edge of Circular Quay, an elegant building developed with Tony Dibden in association with the Arup office which revolved around its central core to share the views Sydney Harbour and cast the smallest possible shadow on the narrow streets of Sydney. An obituary in the NSW Chapter *Architecture Bulletin* recalled Tony's role as mentor to a large body of aspiring architects and his 'quick wit, perseverance and boundless optimism' throughout his twenty-eight years at Hassells.

Stephen and Ursula Conan-Davies, my first residential clients, had lived in exciting places on overseas diplomatic postings and they called their house in Aranda the Boma, a reference to time spent in eastern Africa, where 'boma' means fortress. The house was necessarily quite small but could be, and has been, added to in several directions over the years. Movement was smooth between indoor areas and protected courtyards. We found some more colourful second hand bricks and used them inside and out. The budget was limited and I came up with a simple plan on two levels with a flat roof behind a deep timber fascia. I was surprised in February 1973 when the house appeared with another of my projects in *Cross Section*, the newsletter of the Department of Architecture at the University of Melbourne, which spoke of 'interesting natural material selections, balance of internal spaces and strong chunky forms'. A few months after that there was a lengthy illustrated article on the house in *Australian Home Beautiful* and it was written up in *Architecture in Australia*, the journal of the Institute of Architects. Of all my houses in Belconnen, the Conan-Davies house was for

*Conan-Davies house Aranda 1968*
Byam Wight

many years the best known and it remains a striking object on its steep corner site.

Aranda was the earliest of the new suburbs in Belconnen, the first satellite town north of the Canberra Valley. Land in Aranda slopes down west and north from Black Mountain, with generous buffers of native forest and remnant pastoral land. Residential sites were often quite steep with large mature eucalypts, effectively discouraging irrigated lawns, swimming pools and private tennis courts. This was a time when the Australian bush was acquiring almost spiritual associations. The use of native flora was *de rigueur* in Woden and to all intents mandatory throughout Belconnen, seemingly with an army of environmental activists poised to set upon potential apostates. From its earliest days, Aranda attracted many who worked in the city centre or at the University and were happy to nestle among the trees and live a fruitful life of calm enjoyment.

*Cumpston house Aranda
1973*
Roger Pegrum

One of my largest houses in Aranda was for Helen and John Cumpston. Helen was the first woman graduate in law in Tasmania and a long-time president of the native garden society in Canberra. Her husband was a well-known diplomat and historian and a prolific author on Douglas Mawson and the Antarctic. His contributions to Antarctica—which included assisting with the preparation of the first maps of the continent—were acknowledged with the award of a doctorate of letters from the University of Melbourne in 1949 and the naming of the Cumpston Massif in 1966. The Cumpston house in Araba Street is the nearest house in Canberra to Black Mountain, stepping gently down the hill on three levels with a summer living room and a winter living room and lots of sun. For Helen, there was the joy of tending a real native garden that seemed to go on forever and John got the two-storey library he had always wanted, with a tall ladder on wheels that ran around three sides. When John died and Helen moved to a nursing home, the house was sold to newcomers from Sydney. They employed a Canberra architect (not the one who had defaced Tony's house in Garran but a new man in town) who plastered the place with towers, plastic columns and nasty coloured glass panels. He made no effort to let me know what he was up to and he neglected to remind his clients about their responsibilities under the Copyright Act. I still cannot drive past the site without seething. I was careful not to tell Helen what they had done to their house and I hope she did not hear it from anybody else. I can only imagine how horrified she would have been.

Another simple but dramatic house of mine on a battle-axe block in Hughes (which featured regularly in weekend exhibitions for charity) was drastically altered many years later by another Canberra architect who also forgot to let me know what was happening. A small house of mine in Mirning Crescent has been extended twice in recent years without reference to me, with the architect copying my details and accepting without shame awards from the Institute of Architects for keeping the character and detail of the original. So much, I thought, for moral rights and the old-fashioned ethical framework wherein architects let each other know when they are asked to work on buildings designed by their fellows. One observer said I could have been forgiven for thinking that architects had been hunting down Pegrum houses over the years so they could have their wicked way with them.

In his book *Experiments in Modern Living* Milton Cameron compiled an impressive catalogue of houses built in Canberra between 1950 and 1970 for scientists and academics taking up posts at The Australian National University or with the Commonwealth Scientific and Industrial Research Organisation at Black Mountain. Cameron focused on a handful of fine houses by Roy Grounds, Harry Seidler and Theo Bischoff but I was pleased to see reference also to some of my more modest work, which included houses in Aranda for the Chief of the Division of Plant Industry at CSIRO John Falk and his wife Enid and for the CSIRO entomologist Colin Macdonald and his wife Pam. For the Macdonald house in Mirning Crescent I chose Bowral cream bricks rather than the grey face bricks I more commonly used in Belconnen. A landscaped courtyard at the centre brought daylight into all parts of the house and was connected by an underground pipe to their daughter's bedroom to permit free movement of her pet rat. I was pleased when their daughter Catherine became an architect. She married another Canberra architect, Bruce Townsend, and later became the first woman appointed as ACT Government Architect. Maybe something rubbed off ...

Cameron refers also to one of Tony's houses in Campbell for the economic historian Alan Barnard and to a house

*Wilson house Aranda*
*CS Daley Medal 1974*
*25-Year Award for Enduring Architecture 2005*
Byam Wight

of mine at Wamboin for Gutta Schoefl and her partner Roger Miles. The Schoefl/Miles house was an interesting design challenge. Schoefl was an artist and potter and an experimental neurologist at the John Curtin School of Medical Research. She loved sunlight and asked for a large study with lots of glass. Miles was a mathematician at ANU who didn't like the sun at all and I gave him the dark room he wanted with a high ceiling and a mezzanine. In the middle of the house was neutral ground where the two met for meals and other things. Miles, I was told, worked in the field of geometric chance. One day, while driving out to the site with him, I asked what this meant. Imagine you throw a box of matches into the air, he said, I can tell you about the pattern the matches will make when they land. Good fun, I said, does it have a practical application? Oh yes, said Miles, and the makers of tissues and toilet paper give me all the funding I could ever need to help them make their papers strong or soft or both. He was not a talkative fellow and I did not learn much more about him, but the house looked nothing like a pile of sticks.

Hubert Roetzer built the house I designed for Peter and Raylee Wilson in the same street as the Macdonald house. Peter was a gifted diagnostician with a general medical practice in north Canberra and he and his family were ideal clients. For a short time in the 1980s the house was owned by Canberra architect Candida Griffiths, who had grown up in a house designed by Roy Grounds for her father Philip Griffiths, a renowned soil physicist and poet. In 1974 the Wilson house received the Institute's CS Daley Medal for Architectural Merit. The awards jury that year was chaired by Roger Johnson, newly appointed as the foundation head of the School of Environmental Design at the Canberra College of Advanced Education, and included Melbourne architect Daryl Jackson and Anne Powell, whose husband was NCDC Commissioner Tony Powell. Roger Johnson became a lifelong friend and mentor and, like Peter Harrison, a personal and professional point of contact in Canberra after I had moved to Sydney.

The Wilson house, like many houses in Aranda, backs onto a bushland reserve. The floor plan is split level and

*Lewis house Garran 1969*
Roger Pegrum

follows the sloping site through an informal native landscape garden. It was a large house for the time, but the Z-shaped plan reduces the apparent bulk from the street. There were four bedrooms plus a fifth bedroom/study with an external door, which allowed it to be used as an emergency medical surgery. The lofty living room has a brick fireplace with a generous raised

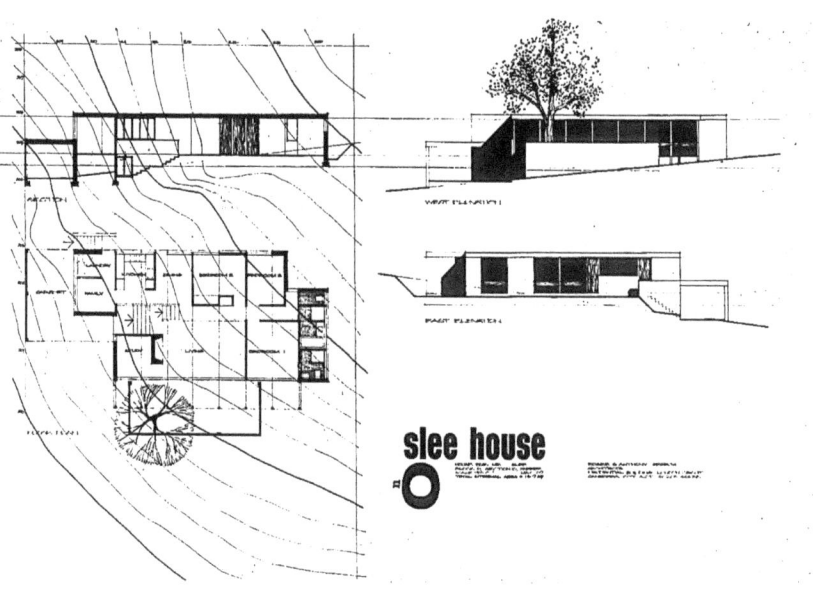

*Slee house Farrer 1969*

hearth and hinged steel arms for slow cooking then and now. Extensive workshop and underfloor storage areas are directly accessible from the garage. I was delighted when the Wilson house was included in the Institute's Register of Significant Twentieth Century Architecture, where it is described as an example of the Sydney Regional Style of architecture, 'informal in character although carefully contrived ... the quality of the house and its siting make an outstanding contribution to its suburban environment'. After coming back to Canberra in 1986, I added a guest room, a spa room and a dressing room and completed a number of other modifications. In 2005, the house received the Institute's 25-Year Award for Enduring Architecture. A renovation of an original bathroom also won an Institute of Architects commendation and was Bathroom of the Year in the Master Builders Excellence Awards in 2014.

Away from the hotbed of upper Aranda, the first of my houses built by Hubert Roetzer was for Tony and Margaret Lewis in Garran, not far from my own house. It was on a single level in bagged and painted brickwork with a flat roof projecting as a verandah on all sides. A Roetzer house never cracked; bricks were always well wetted before laying which allows the mortar to gain strength over several weeks. Hubert's understanding of traditional construction did not prevent him responding positively to advances in materials and techniques when they were offered. I recall him telling me that the painter was about to start work at the Lewis site and wanted to use a new device called a paint roller. I had been brought up by the Department of Works to believe that paint should be applied only with a nice soft brush, but I was smart enough to tell him to go ahead.

The Price house in Gouger Street Torrens was another fine Roetzer product. Like the Macdonald house, it was built around a central courtyard and there was marvellous light in all parts of the house. Roetzer also built a house high on a hill in Waite Street Farrer for Mike and Judy Slee. It was a simple plan on two levels with a quiet and pleasant study for each of them and wonderful views of sunsets over the Brindabellas. When I visited the house twenty years later, almost the only change was Macintosh computers instead of IBM golf ball typewriters. I have since added a new kitchen and family room for the present owners Robert and Cathie Harris. Two other early houses in Farrer have fared well in the care of subsequent owners.

*Kindergarten and Day Nursery Garran 1972 (Canberra Hospital under construction in the background)*
Roger Pegrum

The Lancaster house in Steinwedel Street was given an internal makeover some years ago but retains its street presence and its outstanding outlook down the Woden Valley. The Boldeman house in Woodgate Street is beautifully preserved and sits within a wonderful garden that has been part of Canberra's Open Garden program for almost thirty years.

I was fortunate to have a wide range of other clients including the ACT Totalisator Agency Board, for whom I designed betting shops in all parts of town, including a major outlet on Civic Square on the site of what is now the ACT Legislative Assembly, a strange provenance indeed. Ken Woolley asked me to look after the construction of a classy block of apartments in Garran and I built a soft drink factory in Queanbeyan and a house in Moree for Ralph Hunt, the Minister for the Interior. I designed a clubhouse and other facilities for a new golf course at Narrabundah, using recycled hardwood for footbridges over gullies and consulting my children's books for help with the

*Aged Persons Units Garran 1972*
Byam Wight

design of stiles over fences. For the Canberra manager of Stegbar, I built a pleasant kindergarten and day care centre in Garran with a curved garden wall reminiscent of Thomas Jefferson's brick walls at the University of Virginia.

Rear-Admiral Sir Morgan Morgan-Giles was a member of the House of Commons who visited Canberra in 1970. He called into the office one day seeking advice on the restoration of a large barn at Lake Bathurst near Goulburn. I had planned to be in England later in the year for the birth of our third child, so I delivered my sketches and had lunch with him at the Palace of Westminster in early December. Part of the service, I said, thanks for the lunch. The Commissioner for Housing engaged me to advise him on new designs for public housing and later commissioned me for the first development in Canberra of housing for the active elderly at Garran. I was attracted to the term 'active elderly' and my houses have allowed wherever possible for ageing in place. In 1973, I was awarded the RAIA Hardboards Australia Scholarship for the study of housing for the elderly. I travelled to the United Kingdom, the United States, Denmark, Finland and the USSR and my report was published as *The Architecture of Old Age*.

There were steady offers of work from the NCDC and the Department of Works and we were known for the thoroughness of our construction documentation. We prepared working drawings, specifications and tender documents for several buildings designed by the Department on behalf of the Commission, including laboratories for the CSIRO in Yarralumla and the fire station at Canberra airport. We had a lot of fun with the fire station. The functional brief called for the fire crew to be in the fire truck and out the main door in no more than 45 seconds, at any time on any day of the year. The brigade had the most modern fire trucks at the time, with electric sump heaters so they would start at once on the coldest of days. Large glazed doors facing the runways would normally be kept shut but had to be raised by electric motors within the 45 second limit. If for any reason the doors did not to open in time it had to be possible for the trucks to drive through from a standing start. There was quite a crowd of onlookers and lots of cameras when we tested this on site by setting up a full-size tilt-a-door and then driving a fire truck straight through it.

Early in 1972, the National Capital Development Commission approached me to design shelters for police officers standing guard at the Soviet and Yugoslav embassies. Police had been issued with long woollen underwear for winter, but rain and frosts and unavoidable calls of nature made life uncomfortable for the officers on duty. The regular visit of a mobile toilet inside a Kombi van was the butt of many jokes. The embassy of South Africa was also being picketed at the time and shelters were needed for police on State Circle. The police boxes remain my smallest buildings ever, with a floor area of just over two square metres, glass walls and doors on all sides and with generous roof overhangs. We also poured concrete slabs at likely trouble spots outside a number of embassies and diplomatic residences and cast in bolt holes to secure the corners of the boxes, which were prefabricated in a Queanbeyan factory. There were hooks on the roof and a

*Cartoon by Larry Pickering*
The Canberra Times
*26 September 1972*

fully fitted-out box could be lifted onto a truck and delivered and secured on site in an hour or two. It was an interesting exercise in design and construction. The boxes popped up everywhere and I designed smarter versions with double glazing and electric heaters for the Prime Minister's Lodge. Later still, the boxes were standard items at military bases across the country and many remain in use for other purposes. In far south Canberra, the greyhound track used a retired guard box as a ticket office for many years. Tomorrow's fish and chips ...

The NCDC brief for the police boxes said that they should not look like bus shelters or telephone boxes but inevitably people were found lingering near an empty box. Soon after the first boxes appeared, a cartoon by Larry Pickering in the *Canberra Times* had a burly policeman telling two small children 'Sorry son, I'm right out of Crispies and Paddle Pops ... the only thing I can give you is a smack in the ear'. The Police Association was not amused and a letter to the editor said the cartoon was in 'extremely poor taste'. A 'policeman's wife' wrote that it was 'a slight on all police officers especially those with children of their own'. Amazing that these tiny buildings attracted media interest at all. This would happen again twenty-five years

"Sorry son, I'm right out of Crispies and Paddle Pops ... the only thing I can give you is a smack in the ear".

*Federal Police guard boxes Russian Embassy and Prime Minister's Lodge 1972-73*
Byam Wight

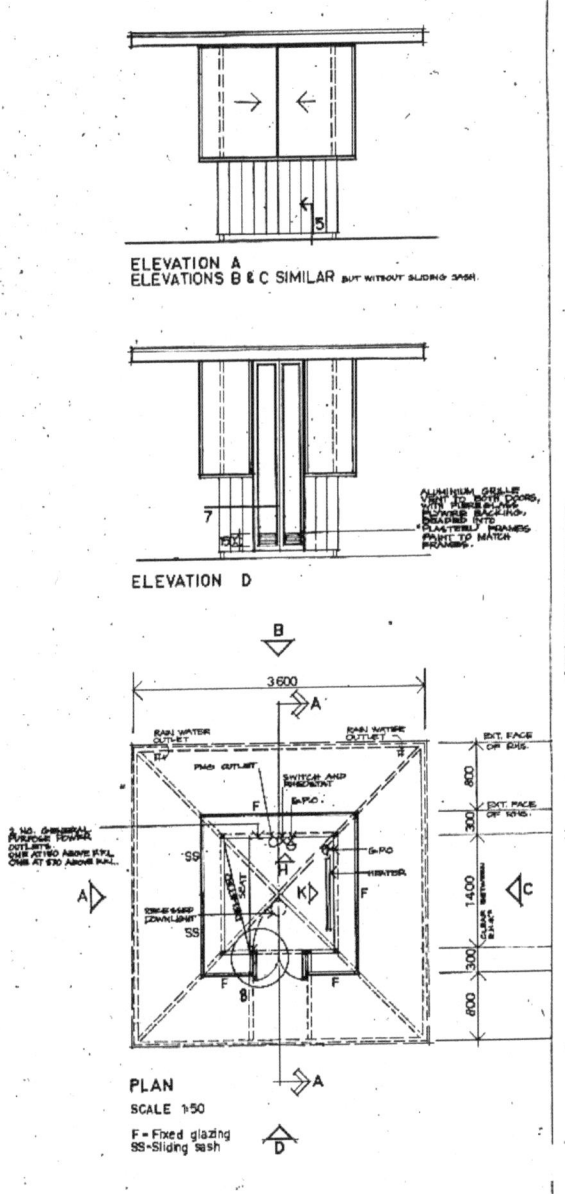
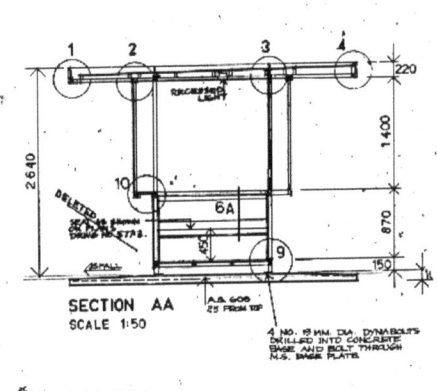
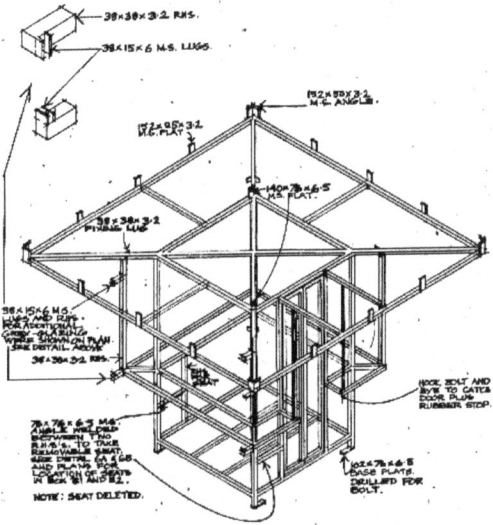
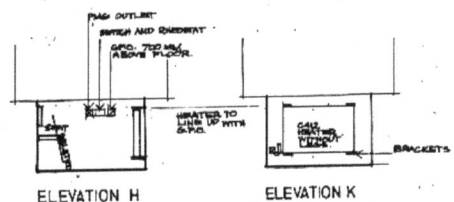

Police Guard Boxes for Commonwealth Police, Prime Ministers Lodge, Canberra — Roger Pegrum Architect, Thetis Court Manuka A.C.T. tel. 950329. For and on behalf of the National Capital Development Commission. Drawn: Liisa. Scale: as shown. File: 577. Date: dec. 1973. Drawing no. 577·2.

Typical Plans Elevations & Sections.

later with the Chancery building at Government House, this time with a cartoon by Geoff Pryor. It was a condition of our engagement for the Chancery that we not talk publicly about the project, but word leaked as the building was nearing completion and the press wanted to know what the new building would look like. The *Canberra Times* could get nothing useful from my office or from Government House, so they ran a silly story on the front page with a sketch of a building modelled on the Taj Mahal. When the newspaper in due course toured the building and took photographs they were much more generous, talking about it as 'a ship of state' and the 'very model for a modern Governor-General'.

*Cartoon by Geoff Pryor*
The Canberra Times
*15 August 1995*

From early 1970, I wrote a number of articles on design for the *Australian* and the *Canberra Times* published stories on aged persons' housing and fashions in architecture plus annual reviews of the state of architecture in the national capital. After visits to England and the east coast of the United States, I wrote about the new town of Bracknell outside London and the 'company towns' of Columbia and Reston outside Washington DC, comparing their approach to design quality with ours in Canberra. Architecture is public property, I said, with the ability to convey a wide range of feelings. I put the case for excellence in planning and design to be spread evenly across the city—'the success of the ultimate city of Canberra will rely as much on its suburban areas as its urban precincts. It would be very poor form indeed for the future Canberra resident to condemn the urban environment from the steps of a poorly designed house'.

The boom time for Canberra continued and the building industry was stretched to breaking point. Materials were hard to get and construction standards were falling fast. In one celebrated case, the bricks for the new hospital in Woden came out of the ovens at the Yarralumla brickworks in the morning and were built in to the façade that afternoon. The bricks were so hot that the bricklayers had to wear asbestos gloves. The bricks absorbed water as they cooled down and 'grassed' but they also grew bigger and fell off the building many floors in the air, causing all sorts of trouble. At the other end of the scale, residential construction was hindered by shortages of labour in all trades. The National Capital Development Commission invited submissions for innovative building systems which might reduce these delays. It was a knee-jerk response to a situation that had been brewing for some time and it was almost guaranteed to fail. People were asked for their thoughts on prefabricated housing. Some agreed that off-site manufacture might speed up construction but generally the public was not impressed at all, suggesting perhaps that if housing went up quickly it might just as quickly fall down.

I entered the fray with a low-key approach for a system of one- and two-storey houses grouped together with steel-framed walls, factory-built service cores and insulated lightweight wall panels. I enjoyed the research and the design process immensely, but none of my houses were ever built. I had been impressed on a trip to the United States with the word 'condominium', which sounded a lot more interesting than 'home unit', the generic term for an apartment in Australia at the time. I manufactured the name 'condomaxium' which I thought was a striking product name and sounded like it promised modern housing that was attractive and bigger than normal. I was attacked from all sides and told I was ruining the roots of the word 'condominium', somebody saying that the name sounded like 'houses for big pricks'. Unsurprisingly, the NCDC played it safe and settled on a system of precast concrete panels, which depended on repetition and mass production and practically guaranteed an emphasis on cost rather than amenity or charm. The precast panels went up in short time on the first project, but it was pulled down within a few years and there was no second or third project.

*A Busy Little Chapter*

My involvement with the activities of the (then Royal) Australian Institute of Architects had begun almost as soon as I graduated and has continued for more than fifty years. The Institute was formed in 1930 when architectural associations in each of the States became Chapters of a new national body. An area committee within the New South Wales Chapter looked after the interests of Canberra until 1962, when an ACT Chapter was formed to represent the growing number of architects in private practice and government employment. The first President of the ACT Chapter was Malcolm Moir, after whom (together with his architect wife Heather Sutherland) a Chapter award for residential architecture is now named. Moir was followed

*Condomaxium prefabricated housing 1973 (project)*

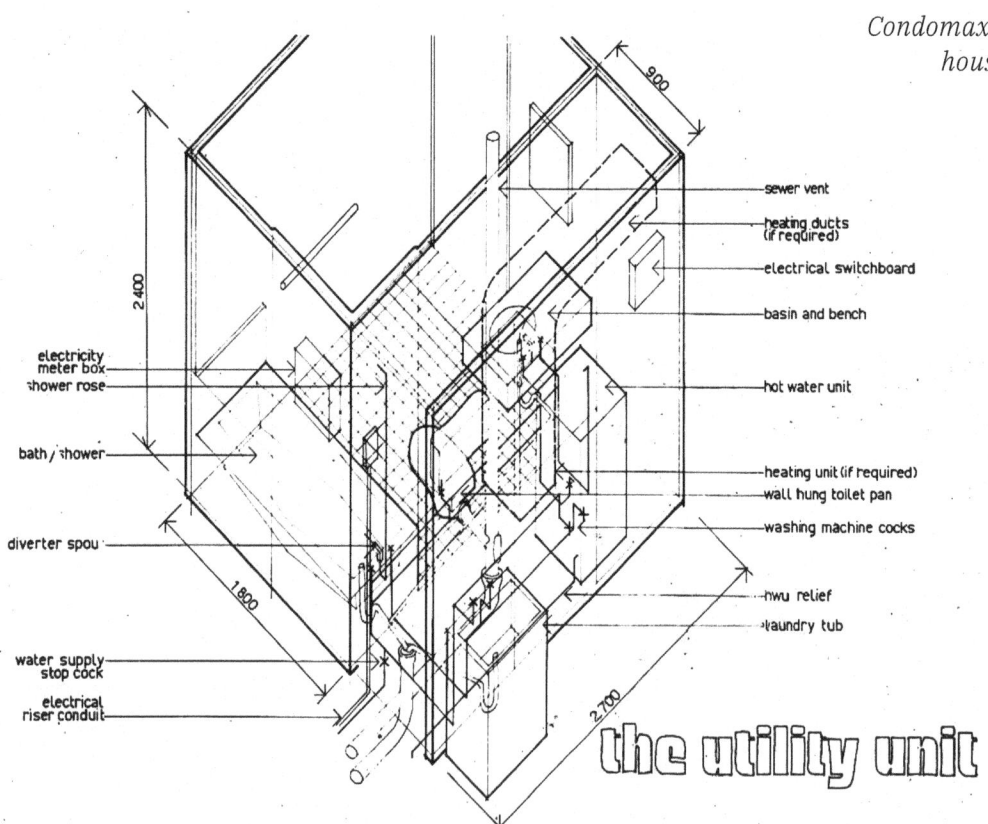

*Telecom Tower
Black Mountain ACT
under construction c.1975
Department of Works ACT
Region and Central Office
Richard Ure, Charles Bubb, Dick
Roennfeldt*

as president by many of Canberra's leading architects of the 60s and 70s—John Scollay, Peter Harrison, John Goldsmith, Horrie Holt, Arthur Tow, Neil Renfree, Tony Cooper and Mervyn Willoughby-Thomas.

Horrie Holt drafted me on to the Council of the ACT Chapter in 1963 as honorary treasurer (there was very little money to worry about). We were a busy little Chapter. We had film nights, exhibitions of Danish furniture and silverware in the new Monaro Mall and tours of new embassies and university buildings. There were regular debates in the *Canberra Times* about architecture and design and we organised weekend exhibitions of recently completed houses by local architects such as Rudi Krastins, Theo Bischoff and Dirk Bolt. We didn't always get it right. In the early 1970s, there were proposals for a telecommunications tower on Black Mountain which would include viewing galleries and a revolving restaurant. The ACT Chapter joined forces with a self-styled Canberra Citizens' Committee To Save Black Mountain and told the Public Works Committee that Canberra architects thought the designs was an eyesore. The wheel has turned sufficiently, I believe, that architects and citizens generally will now rally to save our own Eiffel Tower, a marker to visitors that they have reached their destination and a reminder that Canberra was here before the internet and satellites. The Institute of Architects also appeared at an Enquiry by the Joint Committee on the Australian Capital Territory into employment opportunities in the ACT, where we argued in Parliament House that Canberra architects and engineers should be considered for a greater share of the work going at the time to consultants flying in every morning from interstate with rolls of plans. Perhaps this is yet again a legitimate concern, if not for the same reasons. Certainly not every recent proposal by out-of-town developers shows the understanding and care the city and the community deserves.

I was vice-president of the ACT Chapter for a while and took on the role of promoting architectural awards in Canberra. The principal (and for a long time the only) design award in New South Wales was the Sulman Medal. First given in 1932, it was named for Sir John Sulman,

*Canberra Medallion*
*ACT Chapter RAIA bronze*
*medallions 1969*
Peter Swalling

a prominent Sydney architect who was chairman of the Federal Capital Advisory Committee from 1921 to 1924. Prior to the creation of a separate Chapter of the Institute in the ACT, early Canberra buildings such as the Institute of Anatomy and the Australian War Memorial would have been eligible for consideration for the Sulman Medal but there were few local architects to push their claims. The tables were turned in the 1950s when Canberra dominated the NSW awards with four Sulman Medals. The Royal Swedish Legation in Yarralumla by Peddle, Thorp and Walker and EGH Lundquist became the first Canberra building to win an architectural award of any type when it was awarded the Sulman Medal in 1952. The following year the Medal went to Brian Lewis for University House and in 1955 it was the turn of the Department of Works to win the Sulman with Ian Slater's Olympic Pool in Civic. In 1959, Roy Grounds' iconic Academy of Science was the last Canberra building to be awarded the NSW Sulman Medal. Two years later, the Academy entered the history books when it was awarded the first Canberra Medallion and thus became the only building to be awarded both the Sulman Medal and the Canberra Medallion.

The Canberra Area Committee of the Institute had established an Award for Meritorious Architecture which was marked by a small rectangular plaque screwed to the building. Now that we were an independent Chapter, we spread our wings a bit and changed the name to the Canberra Medallion. Two houses in this period by Sydney architects were awarded the Medallion—an elegant house in National Circuit Forrest by Peter Keys in 1962 (later demolished) and a truly lovely little white house still in original condition from 1965 by Russell Jack high on Mugga Way for Canberra solicitor Mick Cater. We decided to strike a decent looking bronze medal like the Sulman and the present Canberra Medallion was designed by Peter Swalling in my office. The NSW Chapter later introduced a new Wilkinson Award for residential work and in Canberra we followed suit with the CS Daley Medal, a new award for housing. The first CS Daley Medal was awarded in 1968 to Noel Potter of Bunning and Madden for his international style house in

Yarralumla for Professor A J Birch, the Australian organic chemist commonly regarded as the father or perhaps the grandfather of the contraceptive pill.

Awards for architecture in Australia started at about the same time as the better-known awards of the Academy of Motion Picture Arts. As with the Oscars, Canberra's architectural awards are generally well received by the profession and the public but there have been some surprises and disappointments. From time to time, Territory or Commonwealth government buildings fail to gain recognition in Canberra, which should send ripples of concern through the relevant bureaucracies but is most commonly quietly filed away. The Institute's own headquarters building on Mugga Way received no award at all when it was first built, although it was given a 25-Year award in due course. The interior of a small cafe in the Manuka Arcade won the Canberra Medallion in 1996 but everything disappeared in the inevitable upgrade not long after. More than fifty Canberra Medallions have been handed out since 1961, to architects well known and not so well known. However, in ten of those years, the ACT Chapter has given no Medallion at all, which I have argued sends strange messages to our clients (no Oscar for best actor or screenplay or musical score? no Miles Franklin Award?).

In 1995, our Chapter was ahead of the pack when we introduced a 25-Year Award for projects 'that have stood the test of time'. I was put in charge of the jury for its first airing and I asked Peter Freeman and Donald Dunbar to join me. It would be good to launch this with a bang, I said, so we gave three awards: to Enrico Taglietti's wonderful library in Dickson; to Dirk Bolt's Butler House in Garran and to University House at the ANU by Brian Lewis. The *Canberra Times* gave us a whole page for good size black and white photos and eloquent testimonials. A small number of Canberra buildings have more than one award mounted at the entrance side by side, rather a nice result for everybody. For many years now, architecture in the national capital has rightly been accepted as the equal of architecture anywhere in Australia and Canberra architects and buildings have been recognised with numerous national awards.

*CS Daley Medal
ACT Chapter RAIA bronze
medallions 1969*
Peter Swalling

By the middle of the 1970s, the landscape of Canberra's new towns was still incomplete and the town centres lacked identity. Belconnen and Tuggeranong in particular were too large to be comprehensible to either residents or visitors. I worked for a month as a consultant at the NCDC with the British town planner Gordon Stephenson on the layout of Kambah and Wanniassa, the first mega-suburbs in the long valley down to the Murrumbidgee. But working with Stephenson turned out to be a depressing experience because his subdivisions lacked all joy or visual interest. There must be more to planning, I thought, than running roads like spaghetti a hundred metres apart along the contours and dropping schools and playing fields at the bottom on old creek beds and landfill sites. The new towns were being designed for motor traffic, not for communities or individuals, roads in all directions for cars but no streets for people. A fashion for mud coloured bricks, brown tile roofs and dark window frames plus an obsession with keeping buildings low to the ground made the new suburbs look worn and weary before they were even occupied.

The National Capital Development Commission had done a great job to get the city going but now appeared to have lost its way, and its commitment to design excellence seemed to be at an all-time low. The new suburb of O'Malley, on the western slopes of Mt Mugga, had been touted as a 'trend-setting suburb of modern designs distinctive and distinguished as fine modern architecture' but the Commission conceded that 'the result to date has been disappointing'. It was not lost on many that the suburb was named for King O'Malley, one of the earliest supporters of an Australian capital city of the highest quality in design and culture. The Commission confessed in *The Canberra News* that 'however much it may wish to see the fine architecture originally hoped for, it is not in a position to provide it'.

It was time for me to move on. My business was going well, at least in the housing market, but I was not impressed at all with the standard of Canberra's commercial buildings and I saw nothing good happening with redevelopment in what were then the 'older parts' of town. I had a feeling there might not be much fun in running a small architectural office in Canberra in the next few years. I made a conscious decision not to become involved with the main chance developers and construction managers then flocking to Canberra. Time was needed for the local scene to find its way again, I thought. Maybe I could come back one day and pick up where I left off.

I toyed briefly with the idea of working with the United Nations on plans for the new capital city for Tanzania at Dodoma and I had been accepted for an urban design degree at Ohio State University. One evening, at an Institute dinner at the Lakeside Hotel on London Circuit, I was approached by Peter Johnson, the Dean of the Faculty of Architecture at the University of Sydney. He asked if I had considered teaching and said he had a position for three years at Sydney. I decided that was what I would do, for a while at least. I was careful not to desert my housing clients and, before I left, I handed each of them over to the excellent care of local architects Neil Renfree and Clem Cummings, both of whom I had known since University.

# The Sydney Years

*Fine Details*

In May 1974, and with some nervousness, I took up a three year appointment as a lecturer in architecture at the University of Sydney. The students were only fifteen years younger than me and I took it all terribly seriously. Frances and I moved with Emma, Isobel and Adam into a pleasant terrace house in Hargrave Street Paddington next door to Don and Marea Gazzard and we settled the children into Woollahra Demonstration School. Sadly, our marriage did not survive the move and Frances and I were divorced in 1978. It was in all other respects a pleasant change from the relative newness of Canberra and I found the eastern suburbs of Sydney both vibrant and friendly. Streetscapes changed along their lengths and around the next corner, but buildings had a fine and varied grain so that they seemed not to crowd each other. Small but carefully planted front gardens and occasional street trees more than compensated for the loss of the narrow footpaths and wide nature strips of Canberra's suburbs.

A lot of well-known architects lived in the area—Neville Quarry, Angus Teece, Terry Dorrough, Douglas Gordon and Bill Lucas—and I was fortunate to work at the University with first class academics and teachers like Ross Thorne, Jennifer Taylor and Col James. I found departmental committees tedious (Sayre's law: 'academic politics are intense and bitter because the stakes are so low') but within other faculties were men and women whose company I enjoyed and with whom I could discuss almost anything. I was well looked after by our faculty bursar,

Robert Stead, who recognised my freshman condition and offered advice just when I needed it. I was surprised and pleased when my brother Tony moved from Adelaide and opened the Sydney office of Hassell in nearby Jersey Road. Queen Street had a pub and a post office, art galleries and cafes, dentists and delicatessens and antique shops. Halfway along Moncur Street was a humble walk-up block of flats at that time playing an eponymous role in the long-running TV adult soap opera *Number 96*.

There was nothing quite like this in Canberra except perhaps at Manuka. Satisfying and sustainable city-edge precincts like Paddington and Surry Hills or North Melbourne are the products of time and of small-scale commerce and community stewardship rather than statutory planning or short-term real estate opportunities. We picnicked and played tennis at Cooper Park and went to the cricket and the football at the SCG and the Sydney Football Stadium. A 389 bus could take us to the tennis at Darling Harbour or the beach at Bondi. At the top of the road was Centennial Park, the focus of all the ceremony of Federation in 1901. For a number of years, I was chairman of the Holdsworth Street Centre, a busy community centre designed by Terry Dorrough and operating also as a public library and an after-school day care centre. We screened 16mm films every week in winter, a chance for nearby residents to meet each other, starting in the first year with *The African Queen* and ending with *Thelma and Louise*. My first-year architecture students built a billycart track there, launched with much fanfare by the Mayor of Woollahra. It distressed me then and distresses me now that people who are in charge of designing or managing new neighbourhoods believe they can bring about this sort of comfortable character and street life overnight. Big blocky buildings with no ground floor activity and parking basements with dark and dangerous entries will never make safe and pleasant streets. Fine grain frontages and land ownership with the capacity for change must be there at the start or they will not be there at all.

I stayed at the University for twelve years and I do not regret any of the time I spent there. It was entirely necessary that I leave Canberra at some point, even though it meant an almost complete break with the practice of architecture. After my father died in 1979, I continued to visit Canberra regularly to see my mother. I also kept across much of the Canberra professional scene and met up whenever possible with old friends and colleagues. I used my time in Sydney not only to teach but also to write in professional and popular journals and I became quite busy in several areas of design and construction. After I discovered that an academic could take time off and leave the country for several months at a time (nobody thought to mention sabbaticals to me during my first five years there) I also visited and taught at universities all over the world, when I learned that maybe we were not so far behind some of the more famous universities and schools of architecture elsewhere.

Over the years, I taught in all of the design studios and developed courses in the science of building construction for the whole five-year architecture program. There was a rude awakening early on when I told my first-year class that I would be delivering a series of illustrated talks about planning and building the great Australian dream of a freestanding house. I have never lived in a house, said one student. He said he was born in a red brick block of flats, grew up in a cream brick six-pack and was at that point sharing a flat with other students on the first floor of a white painted block in Bondi. I learned quickly that I needed to think outside the Canberra box. I took students on visits to big and small buildings under construction in the suburbs and in the city, causing untold trouble for the University with insurance. We looked at farms and country towns to see how climate and topography influenced design and construction. I enjoyed the company of students who shared my concern to build with both humility and imagination. A number of students from that period went on to make significant marks on our cities and towns—Angelo Candalepas, Richard Francis-Jones, Paul Pholeros, Peter Poulet, Peter Tonkin, Philip Thalis, Annabelle Rodowicz (later Pegrum!), Frank Stanisic and others.

I reminded students that good designers see no gaps from concept design to project delivery. It was necessary, I said, to know how things could be put together in order to make architecture. In my view, Miesian dictums like 'less is more' and 'God is in the details' sit well with studies on how to build what you dream and how to do it economically and competently. In the professional degree, I extended these studies into the finer details of building construction and we analysed the techniques of leading Australian architects in executing some of their best work. I wanted to call the program 'Fine Details' but someone said this sounded like a course in needlework or forgery and it ended up with the rather prosaic title of Materials and Methods. At the time, this course in architectural detailing was the only such program offered in Australia or New Zealand and it became known as a unique component of the curriculum at Sydney. Students learned that architects and builders should be on the same side and work easily together, with both of them understanding what they are trying to achieve and the means by which they will get there.

I enjoyed teaching face to face as much for the regular meetings and discussion as for the final design models or essays. I remember being asked to take over the advanced study report of a final year student whom nobody else wanted to take on. I was in part attracted to the task because of the working title of his thesis—'in defence of the 97-pound weakling'—a reference to the Australian strongman Don Athaldo, who became famous in the 1920s for his showmanship and displays of strength. Short and puny as a youth, Athaldo claimed to have built himself up with exercise and a healthy diet. His persuasive newspaper advertisements showed a bully at the beach kicking sand in the face of a '97-pound weakling'. At the age of fourteen and a little weedy myself, I had been attracted, as had Clive James, to Don Athaldo's correspondence course and his confident assertions that by using 'dynamic tension' I would be able to turn the tables on the bullies of my world. My non-athletic student turned out to be a delight to work with. At our weekly get togethers we talked about making nice buildings and places and a whole lot of other things that had very little to do with concrete and steel. After you leave university, it is harder to find the time for the mind to wander and grow. You should enjoy it while you can.

Shortly after starting work at the University, I was asked by the *Sydney Morning Herald* to review Leonie Sandercock's book *Cities for Sale*. I wrote about how politics is power and how power over land use can be and is too often misused. The review was given a top spot in the newspaper with a lovely cartoon by Emeric Vrbancich. I thought this was rather fun but one academic in the department (whom I hadn't even met yet) stormed into my room to tell me I had no right to say these things when I wasn't even qualified in town planning. Her anger confirmed my resolve to understand something of planning theory, which my working life so far had shown to be an important precursor to the making of good buildings, and I enrolled at once in the postgraduate course in town planning. I was invited to sit on the NSW Chapter awards jury and I wrote the first of a number of major pieces for *Architecture Australia*, the journal of the Institute of Architects.

The Sydney Morning Herald
*24 January 1976*

My review of the Warringah Shire Civic Centre in Dee Why appeared in *Architecture Australia* in August 1975 under the heading 'Wot, no wardens on the catwalks?', a rhetorical question I found in a long list of generally unflattering ratepayers' comments in the visitors' book. I was a little unconvinced about the severity of the interior spaces and the uncompromising façade but wrote positively of the considerable achievement of the architects in combining industrial scale with delicate detailing in a public building unlike anything the conservative ratepayers of Sydney's northern beaches had ever seen. It was an honest assessment of the building and it seemed to please its architect Col Madigan, who sent me a friendly note on its publication and for all the years after smiled at me whenever we met. Research for other articles took me to Lord Howe Island to write up Bruce Eeles' woodhen breeding laboratory and to Alice Springs to review Philip Cox's resort at Uluru. I met leading architects in all the States and spent time at schools of architecture in Australia and New Zealand on behalf of the Architects Accreditation Council. I certainly saw and understood more of Australia and the region than I would have had I stayed in Canberra.

In 1976, I entered a United Nations Habitat competition for the design of squatter housing in the Philippines, a competition won by the talented New Zealand architect Ian Athfield. It is often said that the best competition outcome for an architect is a second or third prize. You can always say the jury picked an inferior design, you will avoid any nasty post-competition problems and you probably won't have to build anything. The Manila competition was certainly not a good one to win, perhaps with the kiss of death because it had been promoted by Imelda Marcos, then the governor of metropolitan Manila. I discussed my ideas with one of my students, Paul Pholeros, who offered to prepare a sketch of life in my *barangay*. I had formed both respect and admiration for Paul's sensitivity and design skills and Paul went on to demonstrate these qualities in his tireless efforts over many

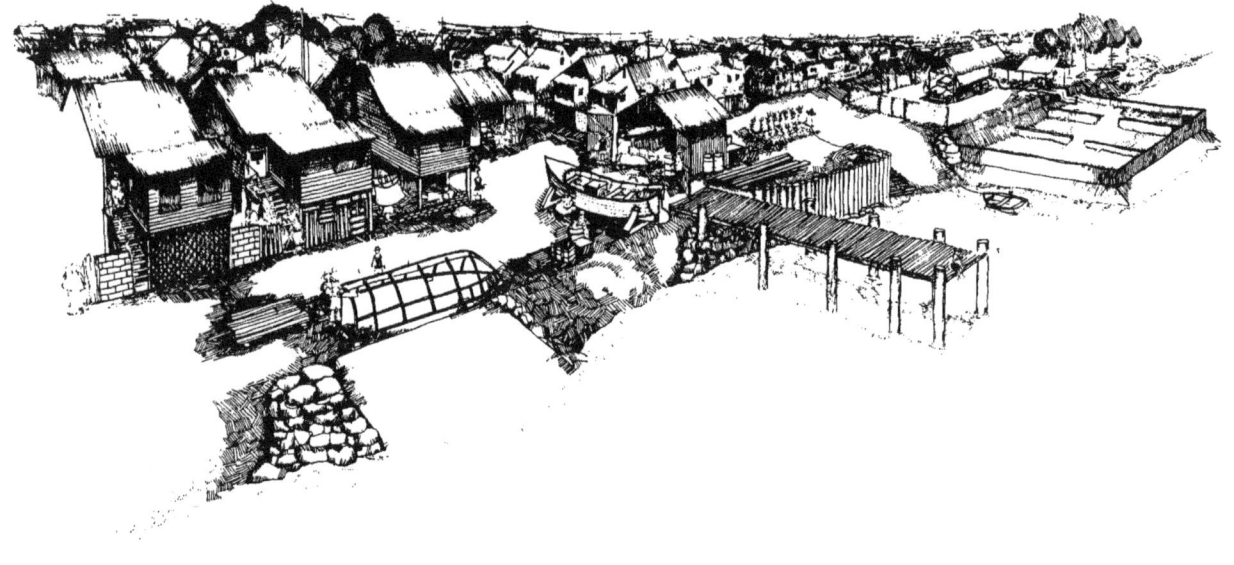

years to improve indigenous health and housing in central Australia. The United Nations competition attracted almost 500 submissions from architects in fifty-two countries, with eighteen entries from Australia. The results were published in 1978 in Michael Seelig's book *The Architecture of Self-Help Communities*. I did not win a second or even a third prize but my design, with Paul's elegant sketch, was the only Australian submission included in the book. Part of Athfield's remarkable and practical squatter *barangay* was erected on the banks of the Longos River but was demolished less than a year later on the orders of Mrs Marcos because she thought 'it looked like a slum'. The unexpected death of Paul Pholeros in 2016 saddened me greatly and left the architectural profession and Australia much the poorer.

I reviewed books from time to time for a number of newspapers and journals and became a good friend of poet and art critic Elizabeth Riddell, for whom I wrote a weekly book review on the letters page of the *Australian*, maximum 500 words, rather fun, like speed dating—'A is for 'Arry Seidler', 'The House that Barry built' and so on. On 9 May 1977, exactly fifty years after the first sitting of the Commonwealth Parliament in the provisional Parliament House in Canberra, the Fraser government announced that the permanent Parliament House would be built on Capital Hill not, as proposed by Walter Burley Griffin, on Camp Hill nor where Holford had said it should be on the southern lakeshore. Known earlier as Kurrajong Hill, Capital Hill is the highest point in the Canberra valley and is at the apex of Griffin's great national triangle. Griffin had seen the hill as the site for an 'isolated Capitol structure ... a dominating architectural feature ... for popular reception ... commemorating Australian achievements' and possibly for the residences of the Governor-General and the Prime Minister.

In 1977, few people were surprised that the politicians had decided to build on the highest point in the valley rather than risk mingling with the tourists and the locals down by the lake, but I was distressed to read that there would not be a competition for the design of Australia's most significant public building. The official announcement of the chosen site was accompanied by much weasel talk of blowouts in time and cost if the design or the architect were to be selected by architectural competition. Joern Utzon's

*Squatter housing Manila, Philippines 1976 Entry in UN Habitat Competition for the Urban Environment of Developing Countries* del. Paul Pholeros

wonderful Opera House had at last opened for business, but the naysayers pointed out as often and as loudly as they could that it had taken a decade and a half to complete and that a public lottery had been needed to pay for it. Instead of a competition to find the best possible Parliament House, it was being proposed that the National Capital Development Commission would choose an architect by means unknown from the ranks of Australia's leading practitioners, one of whom would be asked to sit down with a committee of planners and politicians and come up with a design. I thought the idea was outrageous and I determined to do everything in my power to make sure there would be a proper search for the very best design and the very best architect.

## "THE JOB FOR A GENIUS"

Betty Riddell gave me almost a full page for my strongly worded article 'The Job for a Genius', which appeared in the *Weekend Australian* in August 1977. I made it clear that a great wrong was about to happen unless something was done quickly. I waxed a bit lyrical about combining ceremony with security and technical convenience with spiritual enjoyment in a 'miniature city with a resident population of a few thousand and a floating cast of a million extras a year'. A Committee of the Parliament had visited parliament buildings in Bonn, Kuala Lumpur, New Delhi, Ottawa, Rome and Washington DC and in 1970 had published its findings in a so-called 'Blue Book'. The brief would be for a building with a floor area of almost a million square feet, which I explained was about eight or nine hectares and equal to twenty good-size football fields. The appointed architect, I suggested, would probably come from the left end of the establishment. He or she need not be an Australian, but it was certain that a well-known person would get the job and that was that.

I argued with some vehemence that architectural design competitions produce more great buildings than disappointments, citing overseas successes like the Toronto City Hall and, closer to home, Griffin's design for the national capital city, the competition for the Australian War Memorial after the first World War and the two-stage competition for the High Court then about to start construction. All that really matters, I said, is that Australia gets the very best building—

'the risk of getting a bad design from a good designer is a large one, even for a nation of gamblers'. Malcolm Latham, an associate commissioner at the National Capital Development Commission, telephoned me at the University first thing on Monday morning. He was very cross and said my article was 'unhelpful' and 'needlessly inflammatory'. He particularly chastised me for talking about the size of the building in terms of football fields and he got very short when I told him that Australians knew a lot about football fields but were less familiar with hectares and would be plain frightened at the thought of a building with an area of a million square feet. Rather pompously, Latham told me that a parliament house was a 'very simple building' and he repeated that a competition was quite unnecessary. But I received many calls congratulating me for my stand, which attracted the interest and support of many in Canberra and almost everybody in the architectural profession in Australia and elsewhere. The Clayton's competition put up by the government and the NCDC was quietly abandoned and the rest, as they say, is history. I am pleased to think I played a part in bringing Romaldo Giurgola and his wonderful team to Canberra together with the incomparable talents of Australian artists and designers whose work on Capital Hill has lifted the hearts of us all.

At about this time, Chris Freeman moved from Canberra to Sydney with the Australian Government Overseas Information Service. Chris introduced me to Jim Macdougall, the veteran Sydney journalist who had a weekly column in the *Australian* sponsored by Cathay Pacific Airways. Cathay had just opened a new route from Sydney to London via Hong Kong and Dubai and Macdougall sent me off to the United Arab Emirates to write about life on the Arabian Gulf. Dubai was at that time still quite unique, as yet unspoiled by its looming oil wealth. Known to expatriates as either the Paris of the Middle East or a hardship post or both, Dubai was truly a jewel in the Gulf with gold *suqs* and vast and magical fish and fruit markets. It was a fascinating introduction to a culture and a physical environment I had not seen before but the heat and humidity was suffocating. The locals told me that if you listened carefully you could hear the rust eating your car. I played golf on the desert sands with a square foot of astroturf to put under brightly-coloured balls and the greens were called browns because they were top-dressed with (what else?) crude oil. Macdougall published three of my articles in the Cathay in-flight magazine *Discovery*. The loss of the traditional urban and desert fabric of the Gulf States since that time makes my commentaries read like ancient histories. I have never been back to Dubai.

When Don Dunstan became editor of *POL* magazine in 1980, he approached me to write a number of articles on architecture and design. I reviewed the High Court when it was completed in Canberra and there were major pieces on Philip Cox, Robert Dickson, Peter Corrigan and Maggie Edmond. I was also invited to write the entry on Daryl Jackson in Muriel Emmanuel's 1979 compendium *Contemporary Architects*. In 1980, I made the first of several study tours to the United States and Great Britain and was a visiting tutor and guest lecturer in schools of architecture at the University of New Mexico, City University New York and the University of California at Berkeley.

I gave public lectures on Australian architecture and the planning of Canberra at Portsmouth Polytechnic, the University of Edinburgh and the University of Manchester. On the way home, I stopped off in Damascus, staying for a few delightful days with Neil Truscott, the Australian ambassador to Syria, Lebanon and Jordan, and his lovely wife Claire. The Truscotts and their daughters Marilyn, Janice and Debbie had moved into McKinlay Street at the same time as the Pegrums and our families became firm friends over the years. Neil had arranged for me to give an illustrated talk about Canberra, not yet a century old, in the centre of Damascus, one of the oldest continuously inhabited cities in the world. It was a daunting experience. My address to a huge gathering at the University was translated hesitatingly into French and took more than two and a half hours in what must have been the hottest hall in the Middle East.

*The China Tea Club*

I completed the degree of Master of Town and Country Planning in 1978. My thesis 'The Politics of Planning' delved into the fascinating and sometimes murky stories of politicians and dreamers in the years immediately before and after the federation of the Australian colonies in 1901. In particular, I focused on section 125 of the Constitution and the process of selection of a site for the seat of government of the new Commonwealth. I later offered my thesis as a book to Sydney University Press, but they politely turned it down, as did a number of other academic and commercial publishers. A letter of rejection from George Allen and Unwin said they were 'not sufficiently optimistic about the market' and could see only 'a comparatively small core of Canberra watchers actually buying the book'. A few years later, this was shown to be a bit off the mark. In 1982, at the suggestion of Henry Plociennik and Beth Kennedy, I took the thesis and a draft chapter to Hale and Iremonger, a small publishing house in Marrickville with a reputation for quality titles in fringe areas. With the enthusiastic support there of Sylvia Hale and Lee Shrubb, *The Bush Capital: how Australia chose Canberra as its Federal City* was printed in hard cover and with a large print run. It was launched at the National Gallery of Australia by veteran Labor politician Fred Daly on Canberra Day in 1983, exactly seventy years after the naming of the city in 1913 by Lady Denman, the wife of Australia's first Governor-General.

The book received excellent reviews in major Australian newspapers and magazines and a number of positive endorsements in overseas journals. Manning Clark wrote in the *National Times* that 'any issue which excites rivalry between Sydney and Melbourne is certain to uncover some of the madness in the human heart' and he said I had told the story 'with dignity and restraint'. Writing in *Quadrant*, Edward St John said I had 'done the state some service in writing this loving and detailed account of the long and tortuous process by which the government and people of Australia arrived at the choice of a site and the design for the national capital'. In the *Bulletin,* Edmund Campion wrote that 'Pegrum negotiates successfully the Beechers Brook of Australian history—how our federal Constitution was made'. In the British weekly *New Society*, influential cultural critic Reyner Banham said that I had 'divertingly chronicled the not very edifying process' of site selection although he made it clear that, to his mind, Canberra was still 'a place that nobody wants'.

There was a minor boom of public interest in the early history of Canberra and the critical success of the book played a part in my promotion to associate professor at the University. *The Bush Capital* was serialised in the *Canberra*

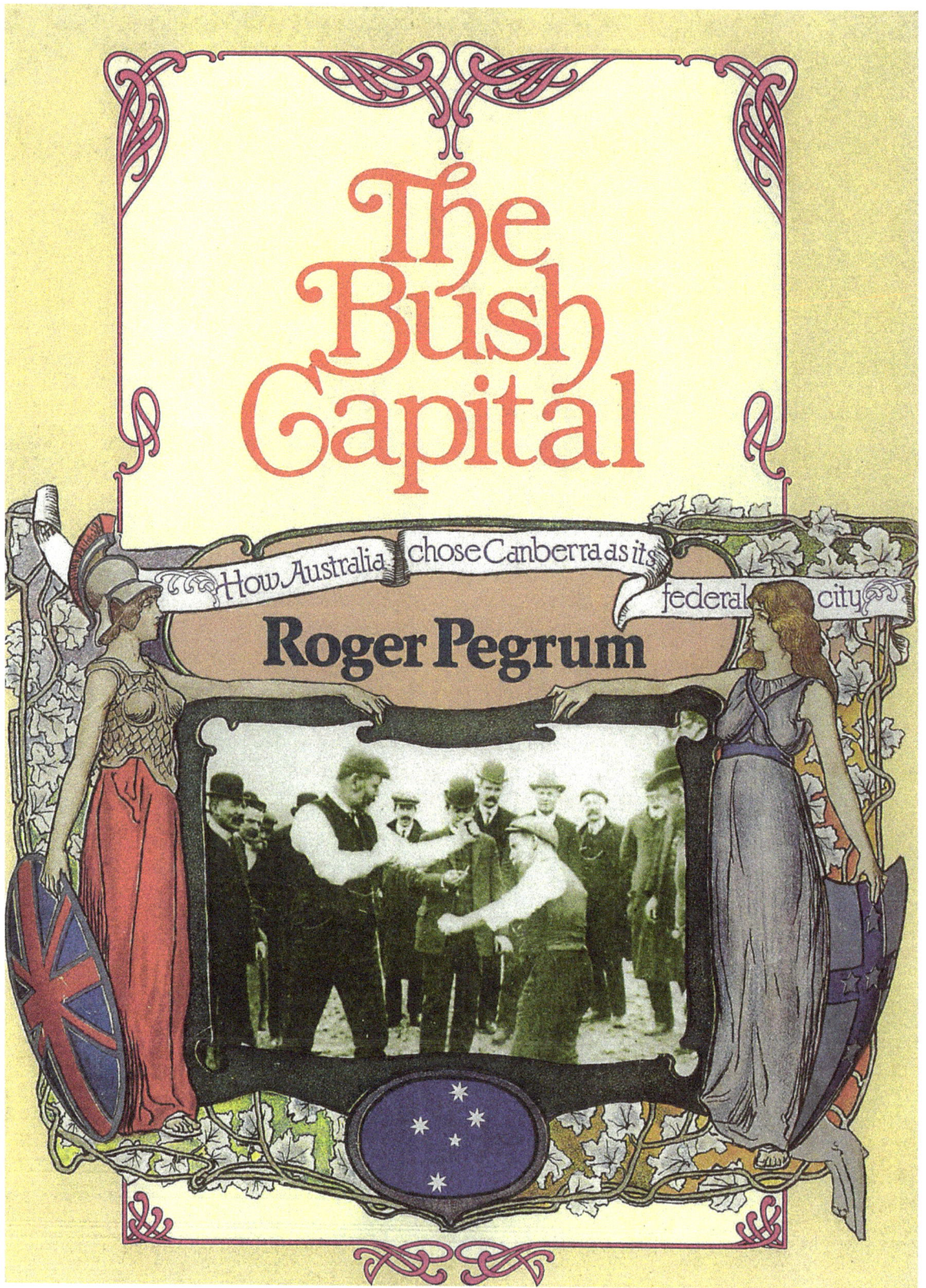

*Times* and featured in the continuing education series *Aspects of Architecture* broadcast by Channel Seven television. I appeared on the *Mike Walsh Show* on the Nine Network before a packed audience with lunchboxes and loud music and choreographed clapping and canned laughter, plus background archival film of the naming of the city in 1913 and Nellie Melba singing at the opening of the Parliament in 1927. A book club sold many thousands of copies as its book of the month and I had the rare thrill for two years of paying provisional tax on royalties.

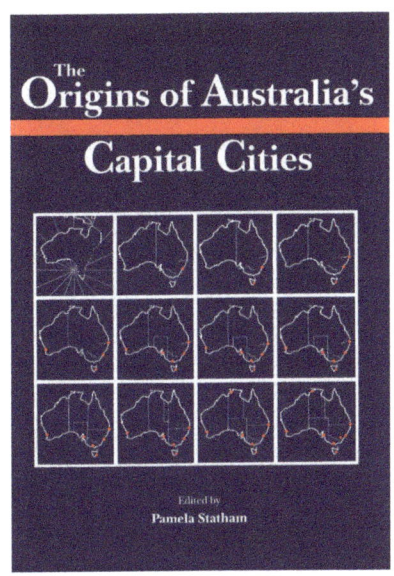

The name 'Bush Capital' has since become associated with all that is good and not so good about Canberra. I became an accidental authority on the birth of Canberra and the work of Walter Burley Griffin and others in the early years of the twentieth century. I was asked to write the chapter on Canberra in Pamela Statham's book *The Origins of Australia's Capital Cities*, which was published in 1989 by Cambridge University Press, and I still give talks on the beginnings of Canberra to students and community groups. I endure a running squabble with one surly journalist who argues that I paid insufficient regard to the boundless charms of Dalgety on the Snowy River and, for some years, Hope Hewitt also attacked me because she said I had ignored the role in the selection of the site played by John Gale, the founder of the *Queanbeyan Age* newspaper. The centenary of the surrender and acceptance of the land for the federal territory in 1908 and the naming of Canberra in 2013 saw the publication of a new edition of *The Bush Capital* by Watermark Press, in colour no less. In an epilogue to this second edition I expressed my abiding admiration for Griffin's Canberra legacy—'in a Chicago winter ten years later, and for a site he had not seen, Walter Burley Griffin found a way to lay out a city 'like no other', a city which is more like a landscape painting that a town plan, perhaps the most outstanding landscape composition Australia will ever see'.

While turning the thesis into a book, I had been introduced by Lee and Peter Shrubb to a small group of Sydney authors and poets who met occasionally for lunch at the China Tea Club in the city. I felt a bit inadequate in the company of these successful people, but I was pleased to be included in their discussions. Among them was Tony Morphett, who had created numerous popular television series including *Blue Heelers*, *Dynasty* and *Water Rats* and who was established as one of the most successful writers in the Australian film and television industry. Remarkably, Tony and I had first met almost thirty years before when I was at Canberra High School and he was a student at Parramatta High School. The two schools competed year about in Canberra or Parramatta in athletics and debating and in a number of team sports. It was our turn in 1954 to go to Sydney where I was billeted with Tony Morphett's family. I was third speaker in the Canberra debating team and Tony was third speaker for Parramatta. Neither of us can remember the subject of our great debate in Parramatta Town Hall that year, but the hometown audience cheered and rolled in the aisles for all of Tony's three minutes and Parramatta romped home. He knew even then that you will win a public debate if you can make the audience laugh out loud. Tony could tell the tallest stories and the most fearful fibs with a perfectly straight face. I suppose it was inevitable that his astonishing way with words would lead to an outstanding career as a storyteller.

Through the 1980s I continued my association with the Institute of Architects, which had established an Education Division in Canberra under the creative leadership of John Dean. John steered the Institute's first venture into publishing with a series of monographs under the title *Australian Architects*, beginning with a handsome volume published in 1984 on the work of Philip Cox, for which I wrote the critical essay 'From Tocal to Yulara'. The book was a finalist in the 1985 Australian Book Publishers Association Awards and was expanded and re-published in 1988 as *Philip Cox, Richardson, Taylor and Partners*, for which I provided a second essay 'From Yulara to Darling Harbour'. Philip sent me a note of thanks and called my words 'flowers of poetry'. The *Australian Architects* series continued with the work of Ken Woolley and, later on, with Rex Addison, Lindsay Clare and Russell Hall. In 1988, I was able to arrange publication of a final book in the series, *Australian Government Architects*, for which I commissioned important essays by Neville Quarry and Roger Johnson.

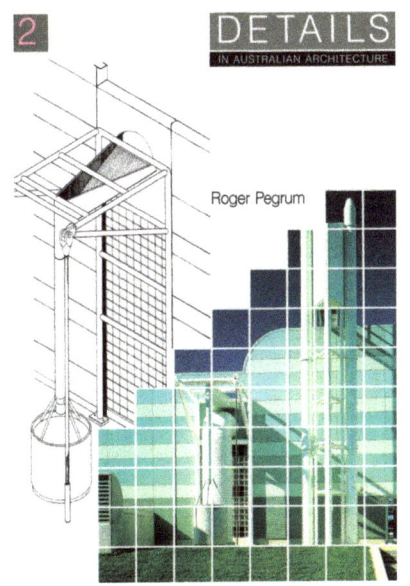

From somewhere within the profession came a rather wild suggestion that the Institute ought to publish an encyclopaedia of Australian building materials and construction techniques. Lecturers in construction were flown in from all over the country for a two-day corroboree at the NSW Chapter headquarters in North Sydney. The meeting collapsed soon after lunch on day one when I said I had heard of moves for a national ban on the use of asbestos in building. It would have been disastrous I said, if this had happened just after the Institute had published a big colourful book showing the wonderful applications of asbestos in award-winning architecture. John Dean proposed instead that I be asked to write a book with photographs and drawings of sound and creative techniques for construction for a target audience of both students and practising architects.

My book *Details in Australian Architecture* was published by the Institute in 1984, cataloguing mainly residential scale works in all States by well-known architects like Lindsay Clare, Louise Kennedy, Ross Feller and Richard le Plastrier. The book was a hit with students of architecture in Australia and New Zealand for many years and extracts were published in *Architecture Australia*. I wrote a follow-up volume *Details in Australian Architecture 2* in 1987 with a wider range of buildings in all States and Territories. I chose not to continue with the series beyond the first two volumes and I remain disappointed that nobody has extended the study of architectural detailing into the brave new world of computer aided design and 3D printing. This could and should still happen, and the quality of contemporary buildings might be much improved in this time of glue-on facades and excessive reliance on software programs designed for convenience rather than creativity.

By the mid-1980s construction was well advanced on the new Parliament House in Canberra and consideration was being given to the future of Murdoch's provisional building below Camp Hill. The National Capital Development Commission engaged leading Sydney heritage architect Howard Tanner to prepare a conservation plan for the old building. I was invited

*View of the Provisional Parliament House and New Parliament House showing the original lighting along Anzac Parade (submitted by Mitchell/Giurgola & Thorp as part of the schematic design phase to the Parliament House Construction Authority during the development of the Parliament House design) pencil on paper vellum drawing by Romaldo Giurgola 1981*
Commonwealth of Australia

to contribute to the study, published early in 1986, on account of my first-hand and detailed knowledge of the building from my time with the Department of Works. My research for the conservation plan established an abiding interest in the work of John Smith Murdoch, who had designed many of the early Canberra buildings that were the backdrop to my life in the fifties. My interest in the provisional Parliament House, without doubt Murdoch's most important public building, would be rekindled a few years later when I was asked to consider how possible future uses might impact on its cultural and heritage significance.

The last of my overseas study tours were to the United States in 1984. In April, I visited the Virginia Polytechnic Institute and State University (Virginia Tech) at Blacksburg—known to the locals as Bleaksburg on account of its isolated position and its harsh mountain winters—where I gave a public lecture on the work of Walter Burley Griffin in Australia. The American Society of Landscape Architects was in town that week for their annual convention. I was lucky enough to get a seat in a packed auditorium on Frederick Law Olmstead's birthday for a memorable lecture by Ian McHarg, whose book *Design with Nature* had made him the godfather of environmental planning. McHarg was a mesmerising speaker and his arguments were delivered with the insistence and quiet power of waves crashing on a beach.

I had arranged to meet with Romaldo Giurgola at the New York office of Mitchell/Giurgola and we spent a fascinating morning discussing the nature of buildings for legislative assembly through history and the special case of Australia's young capital city. In the afternoon Aldo took me with him to Columbia University for a review of graduate work and in the evening we went to the launch of the Rizzoli book *Mitchell/Giurgola Architects*. I also visited I M Pei in his office on Madison Avenue, where he was working on the now-famous pyramid at the Louvre in Paris. Pei had been the only non-Australian assessor in the Parliament House competition won by Mitchell/Giurgola. I gave him photos of the construction work on Capital Hill and he was pleased to be brought up to date with progress. I must say I was surprised when he said I was the first Australian who had come to see him in the nearly four years since the competition.

I wondered at the time if his fame discouraged visiting architects or whether Australians treat the contribution of overseas experts a bit too casually.

I returned to the United States in November, staying with friends in Washington DC before moving north to Boston. Some of the most renowned architects in the world have built in Boston. Harvard University and the nearby Massachusetts Institute of Technology have been described as living museums of architecture in America. I was pleased to spend time in John Andrews' remarkable Graduate School of Design at Harvard, where Peter Corrigan had just completed an appointment as guest professor. The Massachusetts Institute of Technology has the oldest architectural program in the United States. Among its graduates in 1894 had been Marion Mahony, whose marvellous drawings fifteen years later would win for her husband Walter Burley Griffin the first prize in the competition for Australia's national capital city. I had been invited to Boston by the Dean at MIT, John de Monchaux, a graduate of Sydney who had worked with Richard Llewelyn-Davies on the planning of Milton Keynes north of London, a contemporaneous model for Canberra's first new towns of Woden and Belconnen. I was a commentator for end of semester design submissions and my lecture 'On Top Down Under' was the final talk in the MIT Fall Lecture Series. I sat in on several presentations of invented futures which was rather fun (Elderly City? Intelligent City? Fantastic City? Self-conscious City?—some of these projections perhaps unnervingly relevant to Canberra) and I was a guest critic at evening studio sessions at the Boston Architectural Center.

I had been looking forward to my visit to Yale University at New Haven, incredibly well-endowed and considered to have the most outstanding school of architecture in the country. Like many US graduate schools (but unlike most Australian schools at that time) Yale held the view that architecture is primarily an intellectual discipline. Students were assumed to have a sound liberal arts background and entry standards for the professional degree were high. Design work was at the core of the program and all work was centred in the studios which,

*City University New York 1980*

like architecture studios everywhere, were messy and poorly lit. The story of Paul Rudolph's brutal concrete building at Yale was known throughout the architectural world. Students and staff disliked it from the beginning and when Rudolph did nothing about their complaints, the building mysteriously caught fire. At most schools of architecture, criticism is synoptic and constructive and makes reference at least to urban design and tectonics and the practical but essential matters of feasibility and reality. Discussion at Yale focused instead on symbolism, metaphor and imagery, all very absorbing but reminiscent of a glass bead game, rather more Melbourne than Sydney I thought. Tim Culvahouse, one of the students presenting that day, took time out to capture my profile as I absorbed this symbolic wisdom and he presented his sketch to me when the day was over. Maybe he captured my interest in the nature of being, maybe we both missed it.

On the way home, I spent two days in design reviews at the University of Pennsylvania in Philadelphia, sitting with architects from Osaka, Cape Town and Paris. The University of Pennsylvania was a popular destination for Australians and I met up there with some of my Sydney postgraduate students. Design solutions were often of a high standard, ranging from the playful to the serious, but some time was wasted in misreading drawings that had no words on them. It seemed to be some sort of Ivy League/Beaux Arts tradition not to add helpful text or dimensions to the drawings. The results are pretty but who knows what it is and how it all works. Finally, I dropped in on Ohio State University, at the time the largest university in the United States in terms of student numbers. The main campus in Columbus had an airport, two golf courses and its own power plant and offered undergraduate and postgraduate programs in architecture, landscape architecture and city planning. I spent two days in Columbus and attended a number of studio sessions and seminars as guest critic for final year additions to Louis Kahn's Kimball Museum at Fort Worth.

I felt that each of my overseas visits had been a worthwhile investment of time and money. Some conclusions—a degree in architecture should be the product of a university first and a school of architecture second and courses in architecture should foster intellectual curiosity. If this has not happened by this stage of one's life, it is not going to emerge like magic later on.

Roger Pegrum @ Yale 14 Dec 1984 Tim Culvahouse

Ten years after moving to Sydney for what I had thought would be a three-year posting, I was starting to ask myself whether I wanted to stay an academic for the rest of my life or do something different. I thought of moving elsewhere and submitted an application for the chair in architecture at the University of Newcastle made vacant by the retirement of Frederick Romberg. That appointment was deservedly won by Barry Maitland, who went on to turn his school of architecture into one of the best in the land. Barry has remained a good friend and in retirement has become famous as a novelist. I recall at the time telling Peter Harrison of my disappointment in losing out to Barry for the position at Newcastle. Peter reminded me of Winston Churchill's dismay when he lost the UK general election in 1945 after he had guided England through World War II. Clementine told him the result was probably a blessing in disguise to which Winston is said to have replied that 'it was bloody well disguised'.

During my time at the University, I was on occasion asked whether I would ever consider going back to Canberra, to which I replied that of course I would if I had something really terrific to do. That terrific (and totally unexpected) thing was an approach to take up the position of Director of Architecture for the Commonwealth, something I could not possibly pass up.

*Commonwealth Bank Martin Place
Sydney. Architects HE Ross and HR Rowe 1928.
Conservation and refurbishment 1989 Department of Works
NSW Region in association with Devine Erby Mazlin and
Noel Bell Ridley Smith*

# Back to Canberra

*No, you can't, yes I can.*

At the end of April 1986, twelve years after I had left Canberra for the brighter lights of Sydney, I drove back down the highway and re-started my life as Director of Architecture in the head office of the Department of Housing and Construction—the latest of many names for the Commonwealth Department of Works. It was good to be back in town. I was mildly amused by the symmetry of it all—six years in private practice and twelve years as an academic, now back in a city I understood and loved. Canberra turned on sunshine and its finest autumn colours and I moved into an apartment on Brisbane Avenue, a stone's throw from where I had first gone to work as a cadet with the Department.

My departure from the University had been reasonably uneventful. Some kind words were spoken and promises made that were unlikely to be kept. My appointment in Canberra was for three years, and the University gave me a leave of absence and kept open my position as an associate professor. Someone decided to keep my name on the board in the faculty foyer as well. I thought twelve years was quite long enough to stay in one place and I was pretty sure I would not be coming back. I think a few others realised this too. My time at Sydney had seen both change and ossification, and I was not foolish enough to think that the rate of either would change dramatically in my absence.

Writing a last hurrah for the student newsletter *Surryville Times*, I said I would have liked to have seen greater communication among staff and students. Hopefully, I wrote, we were all there because we thought that the pursuit of good design was a worthy cause. Our fees and salaries were paid from the public purse in the hope that we would use our energies wisely, but I regretted that we had not always done this. I hoped the next few years would see wide-ranging debate about things that really mattered. If we did not do this, I suggested, we might find one day that others more powerful than us had decided we did not matter at all. I thanked just about everybody for making my time there worthwhile. My special thanks went to Jack Cowan, who had known me as both student and faculty member and who had become a good friend. He was not always popular with the students but he had never wavered in his concern for scholarship and imagination, two essential components I thought of a good school of architecture.

The University of Sydney operated within a conservative and finely tuned 150-year old bureaucracy, but it had not prepared me for the polished performances I would find in the upper echelons of the Commonwealth public service. My first Departmental Secretary was Tony Blunn, one of Canberra's most respected mandarins, with a distinguished career in public administration and public policy including as Secretary of the Department of the Capital Territory and the Attorney-General's Department. Tony has the rare honour of an Antarctic island named after him for his management of Australia's Antarctic program, the rebuilding of our research facilities there and the return to Australia of the huskies. It occurred to me, in the light of my earlier knowledge of the work of John Cumpston, that Canberra has a special connection with the twentieth century story of Antarctica. Tony called me in within days of my arrival for the first of several fireside chats and set out to tell me the difference between a professional public servant and a professional in the public service. I assured him I had that one worked out before I left Sydney. I did not expect to win any sort of argument with someone who had years of experience in the civil service. What was more, I told him, I would try not to start anything I could not reasonably expect to complete before I left in three years' time. Tony was and is far wiser than any of the clever folk I had dealt with at Sydney and much more fun to be with and we have remained good friends despite having differing views on almost everything. I also learned early not to bet with him when I carelessly misquoted Coleridge and lost a good bottle of Vasse Felix claret.

The selection criteria for the position of Director of Architecture aimed high in hope. The person appointed was required to demonstrate an 'awareness and understanding of public architecture and the profession of architecture generally'. A bit more tricky was the expectation that he or she would have a 'distinguished record of architectural design and a standing in the profession to be able to communicate effectively with his or her peers and provide constructive comment for the enhancement of the skills of departmental architects'. I did not claim the expected record in architectural design, but it turned out that I was favourably regarded for the courses I had run at Sydney University and for my articles and books, and this stood me in good stead in my many meetings and design reviews. Nevertheless, for the next three years I arm-wrestled with the state directors over our conflicting interpretations of 'constructive comment for the enhancement of the skills of departmental architects'. Historically jealous of the power of those in head office to involve themselves in design outcomes, the regional directors generally waited only long enough for my plane to leave the ground before overruling everything I had said to their architects and other technical staff.

The position required me to have a security assessment to top secret, a bit of a heavy load I thought for an architect from a country town lifted from the musty recesses of academia. I found this amusing too since I had on several occasions while at Sydney University been visited by ASIO agents who arrived wearing raincoats (truly!) and looking for dirt (girls or boys or both? drink? drugs?) on Canberra friends under consideration for senior appointments within the Commonwealth. I had not had a medical examination of the cough please type since we were all examined for National Service at age 18, but I had to drop my trousers for the Commonwealth Medical Officer in Civic and be given the once over again. He didn't find anything to worry about and I was even given a certificate saying I was free of AIDS. How many people, I wondered, had one of those in 1986?

*Olympic swimming pool*
*Canberra ACT 1955*
*Department of Works*
*ACT Region*
*Ian Slater*
*RAIA John Sulman Medal 1955*
Australian News & Information Bureau
William Pederson
National Archives

The Department of Housing and Construction was the penultimate manifestation of the Commonwealth public works authority of which John Smith Murdoch had been the first Chief Architect. Murdoch came from Scotland as a young man and had worked as an architect in the Queensland Department of Public Works. At federation, he transferred to the Public Works Branch of the Department of Home Affairs in Melbourne, where he was responsible for providing government buildings and infrastructure across the country—post offices, customs houses, law courts, military establishments and so on. My interest in Murdoch was of long standing but I developed a special fondness for the man who had been the first Commonwealth Architect when I discovered two years later that I would be the last.

Murdoch played a number of key roles in the early history of Canberra and designed many of its first public buildings including the provisional Parliament House, the flanking secretariat buildings and the nearby Hotel Canberra and Hotel Kurrajong. He was an adjudicator in the competition for the design of the Australian War Memorial but had also been a member of the infamous Departmental Board that hacked at Griffin's design so that the powerhouse Murdoch

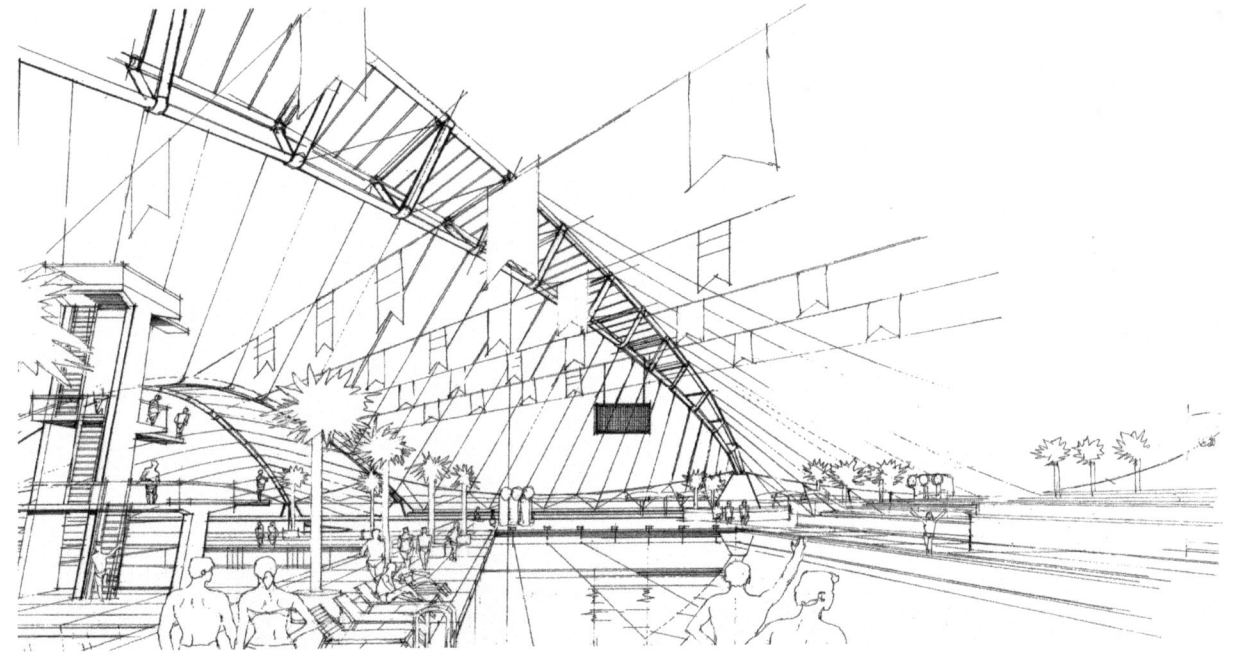

designed at Kingston sits intriguingly askew on its avenue site. Murdoch retired as Chief Architect in 1929 and was followed by Edwin Hubert Henderson. Murdoch had worked within a stripped classical style of architecture but Henderson favoured a more romantic inter-war Art Deco style. In Canberra, Henderson designed the delightful swimming pool at Manuka and the first stage of the National Library in Kings Avenue, where I had spent many long Sunday afternoons in the reading room. One of Henderson's major projects for additions to the General Post Office in Sydney's Martin Place was the subject of a Royal Commission into the issuing of building contracts. The Commission found no fault with Henderson in the matter but he suffered considerably from the ordeal and he committed suicide in Canberra in June 1939.

Following the death of Henderson, his close associate Cuthbert Whitley acted as Chief Architect for some time and completed several buildings he had designed in conjunction with Henderson. One of these was the Patent Office in Kings Avenue, a much-admired formal composition with sandstone facings and restrained Art Deco embellishments. The ambitions of Henderson and Whitley for a truly modern national capital city were demonstrated in their designs for a number of other public buildings including the primary school at Ainslie and my high school at Acton. But the workload took a heavy toll on Whitley. After suffering the first of several strokes, he retired in 1942 and died of a cerebral haemorrhage a month later.

John Overall had been Chief Architect in the Department of Works in Melbourne from 1952 to 1957 prior to his move to Canberra to head the National Capital Development Commission. During the years when I was a graduate architect, the position of Chief Architect in the Department was held by Richard Ure, who enjoyed a high profile in the profession following his win in the 1949 competition for the design of the Australian-American War Memorial at Russell Hill. I recall occasional visits by Ure to our office in the woolsheds when he was ushered from drawing board to drawing board with much ceremony.

Without doubt the most qualified person ever to have been Chief Architect of the Commonwealth was Peter Hall. Appointed in 1977, Hall had an outstanding record of fine buildings within the office of the NSW Government Architect but he is best known for the invitation extended to him to complete Sydney's Opera House after the departure of Joern Utzon. As I have noted earlier, the subsequent vilification of Hall by his uninformed and far less talented peers was unfortunate and unforgivable. Hall's remarkable contribution to the making of Sydney's modern masterpiece was not recognised until 2003, when the Institute of Architects introduced a national 25-year award for enduring architecture and his name was formally attached to the Concert Hall and Opera Theatre for the first time. In his fascinating biography *The Phantom of the Opera House*, Peter Webber describes Peter Hall as 'one of the outstanding Australian architects of his generation ... when Utzon resigned no other was better qualified to rise to the challenge of completing the design of the Opera House'. As Director of Architecture, Hall applied both his design skills and his experience with the bureaucracy to important projects such as the Defence Force Academy at Duntroon which were later recognised with major awards for architectural excellence. The work of Peter Hall was continued by his successor Bruce Bowden, who maintained and enhanced the professional profile of the Department at all levels. His successor and my immediate predecessor was Boris Kazanski, an Australian architect then working in Europe. Appointed on a three-year contract, Kazanski arrived for work in October 1985 but announced at lunchtime on his first day that he was resigning immediately. An embarrassing episode, although I understand that the government was successful in recovering its costs.

I was thoroughly briefed on the work undertaken by the Department, some of it reasonably conventional but much of it demanding dedication and innovation at the highest level. At the University I had no assistants, personal, executive or any other sort. Now I was in the deep end but with many helpful staff to save me. My first line of attack and defence was my three chief architects, each with strong personal and business connections with client departments and agencies. The most senior of these was Athol Richards, a lifetime government architect who had been working in the ACT regional office when I joined as a cadet. Athol had experience in almost every aspect of our operations and I was grateful for his wise counsel. My chief architect for environment and heritage issues was Grahame Crocket, who was working at the time with Garth Setchell on the conservation of heritage buildings at Kingston and Arthur's Vale on Norfolk Island. Their 1988 conservation management plan prepared in association with Clive Lucas was regarded by the Australian Heritage Commission as a model for all future CMPs. Grahame became a particular friend perhaps because we both believed there was such a thing as good design and because we thought similarly about intellectual rigour and clear communication. We have remained close since that time with a number of other common interests including older cars and cricket.

Mike Williams, my third chief, was a talented architect committed to high quality public works and with the challenging task of managing defence programs. Mike told me soon after my arrival that there were problems with one of his smaller projects, a new residence for the commanding officer at the Larrakeyah Barracks in Darwin, whom I recall being at the level of a lieutenant-colonel. A small team of architects and engineers in the South Australia regional office had come up with a building that promised to serve its purpose with some distinction. It was an efficient and attractive design, defying the current fashion in the Territory for low-set buildings on concrete slabs and instead raising the house above the ground with benefits for year-round comfort and amenity in a testing climate. I had met with the designers in Adelaide and knew they would be thrilled to see it all brought to life.

The house was a fraction larger than allowed by the scales and standards for the commanding officer's rank. The Department of Defence had approved the design as it developed but the bad news was that the pre-tender estimate had come in two or three thousand dollars over the agreed appropriation. The brass at Russell Hill told Mike he had to reduce the cost by chopping off the bits not specifically permitted by the scales and standards. Inevitably these were the things (slightly bigger family area, private terrace etc) that would make the place liveable in a Top End environment. I suggested to Mike that if we went to tender perhaps the price might come in within the approved cost and all would be well. Defence would have none of that, so

I asked to meet with them and see if we could find a way out of the impasse. A lot of men (no women) in nice crisp uniforms turned up after lunch one day, ready to fight for as long as it took over nothing very much. Half an hour later, when it became clear that we were going nowhere, I pulled out my chequebook and said that I was being well paid and would be pleased to pay the difference between the estimate and the appropriation and they could pay me back if the money was not needed. To whom should I make out the cheque? This did not compute at all. The meeting broke up in some confusion but within a few days we got their agreement to go to tender as soon as we wished.

In addition to the hundreds of architects in the regional offices, I inherited a whole floor of architects in Canberra with expertise in every aspect of design, project management and construction in urban, rural and remote settings and also in energy conservation, cultural heritage matters and building evaluation. In matters of cost planning, I had the benefit of the advice of Bob Rosenbauer, the Department's chief quantity surveyor. I was fortunate also to get on well with Charles Bubb, the creative and ebullient Director of Engineering, who always had time for me, perhaps because he knew my father had been a civil engineer. I told his happy team on the fifth floor that I had chosen not to follow my father into engineering after I had heard it said that 'bridges, tunnels, dams and piers—that's the stuff for engineers; but wine, fun, song and sex—that's the stuff for architects'.

I remember being never quite sure what Charles thought of architects in general. Early on he told me he had heard of a new definition for risk engineering—'put an architect on the team'. Charles and I were thrown together almost immediately after I arrived when we were directed from somewhere up high to stop rain entering the Cameron Offices in Belconnen. These buildings had been the subject of a highly publicised suit for libel a few years before. Charles and I worked comfortably alongside each other to save the buildings, him grouting all the high tensile steel rods that held the place up and me putting a low-profile metal deck roof over everything to keep out the rain. We gave Cameron a few more years of life, but it in due course met the fate of many buildings ahead of their time but with floor space ratios no longer big enough for superannuation funds and greedy property managers.

Charles Bubb's staff had impressive pedigrees and a storehouse of knowledge in structural and hydraulic engineering, airfield design and military security. His chief mechanical engineer, Clive Broadbent, had earned national and international recognition for his discovery of the link between Legionnaires' Disease and the water-filled air conditioning cooling towers on the roofs of many city buildings. The profession of engineering, Charles once said, is about 'taking risks in the face of uncertainty' and it was this that put him and his fellow engineers at odds with science. In his view, art and judgement made up at least half of engineering practice. It was the lot of engineers, he said, to produce things that work in the real world, 'usually in the absence of sufficient data and sometimes without a really fundamental scientific understanding of why that which must be done works at all'. This, said Charles, is anathema to the scientific mind and the main reason why engineering is not merely a part of science and technology.

In the time I spent with Charles Bubb, I was reminded of discussions with my father in my teenage years and of my later pleasure at working with Murray Northrop, Bryan Cossart, Ron Rogers and other first-class engineers. It has always been fun to meet people who love their work and can take their responsibilities seriously while enjoying life. A lot of folk can't do that because they take themselves far too seriously. Charles Bubb's refreshing views on art and technology came to mind twenty-five years later when the Institution of Engineers (by then known as Engineers Australia) sponsored a forest of Pin Oaks at the National Arboretum in Canberra, engaging Annabelle Pegrum as the competition adviser for a showcase installation among the trees. In other times, this might have produced a sheet of concrete suspended by piano wire or a steam engine made from a recycled submarine but the winning entry by Bligh Tanner from Queensland was based on the cochlear implant, a true marvel of both engineering and science.

I was given a large office high up in the northeast corner of a heavy brick office building on Northbourne Avenue. Bruce Bowden, who had sat in the same room when he took over from Peter Hall as Director, said the principal charm of the room was the splendid view it had of the highway escape route to Sydney. I was gently eased into position and held in place by a personal assistant, John Statton, and was given an executive assistant (a term new to me, nothing like that at university, where were all the secretaries?) in Shorus Kit, who turned out to have been married at some stage to a chap from my final year at Canberra High. John and Shorus were loyal assistants in all my endeavours and I would have been eaten for breakfast without their steadfast support as I set out into what could be enemy territory. Shorus waited patiently during my frequent trips interstate. She gave me a cartoon with herself as the trained wolf and me as the Phantom Ghost Who Walks in striped underpants standing with one hand on the doorknob and pipe in mouth, saying 'hold the fort, Devil, I must slip away once more'.

*cartoon by Shorus Kit 1986*

With the enthusiastic assistance of John Statton and the architects in head office, we resurrected *Architecture In-House*, a quarterly broadsheet on matters architectural, which Bruce Bowden had first produced in 1983. I wrote in the first issue that our job was simple—'to produce public architecture which suits its client and its setting, and which adds to the quality of our environment'. I reminded everyone that, in another age, Professor Leslie Wilkinson had said that it was 'not as important to be in style as to have style'. The work of government architects, I said, should have style and confidence wherever it appears in Australia or overseas. The problems and the settings will be different and so too will be the solutions, but whatever we do must be good. 'Only then', I wrote, 'will our clients understand us and maybe even thank us'.

Soon after my arrival, the ACT Chapter of the Institute of Architects asked if I would organise that year's Walter Burley Griffin Memorial Lecture, which had been presented in the splendid Becker Hall at the Academy of Science for nearly twenty-five years. Nowadays, this is a rather politically correct lunchtime affair at the National Press Club, but it was once a high point in the winter calendars of Canberra's town planning and design fraternity with strong debate and wide-ranging discussion plus drinks and fine food before and after. The first Griffin Lecture had been given in 1961 by Peter Harrison, the inaugural chief planner with the National Capital Development Commission. Subsequent speakers were of the highest standing in their fields—Robin Boyd, Leslie Wilkinson, Gough Whitlam, Roy Grounds (speaking in the building he designed), Hugh Stretton, Roger Johnson, John Andrews, Manning Clark, Sue Holliday, George Molnar and others. It fell to me to find a speaker and I settled on Phillip Adams, known more as a journalist and film-maker than as an authority on design or planning. As one might have expected from the producer of *The Adventures of Barry McKenzie* and *Don's Party*, Adams' presentation on 'The Folly of Architecture' was certainly iconoclastic, even uncomfortable, but it was brilliantly crafted and was well received by those present.

I remember being grateful that Adams had taken our invitation seriously and had given us something to think about. The following year, the Institute extended the invitation to Alan Bond, who arrived late and overdressed with a large entourage, all looking rather lost and missing the whole point of the evening. Bond showed a corporate video, said nothing of real interest and looked all the time at his watch, reminding us constantly that he must soon board his corporate jet because he was off to have breakfast with Ronald Reagan at the White House.

We included a review of Adams' lecture in the next issue of *Architecture In-House*. 'Where were the architects when the ordinary people needed them?', Adams asked, 'architects by and large have opted for the self-gratification that comes with creating monuments to themselves and pandering to the vainglorious wishes of egotistical clients ... architecture has bequeathed a grossly inhumane and largely irrelevant agglomeration of built litter ... whether collaborating in the wilful destruction of the past to provide real estate for their contemporary (and therefore clearly superior) statements or building multistorey filing cabinets for the Housing Commission, architects have been contributing to the humourless, lacklustre and environmental catastrophes of our architectural heritage ... the skyscrapers that are about as different as soap powder packets and the brick veneereal suburbs are a reflection of the anonymity that pervades this crazed and neurotic society'. It remained to be seen, said Adams, whether the present generation of architects were indeed 'heroes of the age' or would prove to carry the baggage of their predecessors: 'just as scientists must redeem themselves by beating their nuclear swords into ploughshares for peace, architects must increasingly change their emphasis and their historical direction'.

I told architects in the Department that we should listen to non-architects like Adams when they have something to say about our work. It was important, I said, 'to stand back from time to time and ask ourselves what we are doing and where we might be going'. I was prompted to these musings, I wrote, 'by a growing concern about design integrity in Australian architecture. So much of what we see is a shallow pastiche of trendy images ... the ubiquitous barrel vault, the almost obligatory curved hoods in corrugated steel, the appalling use of polycarbonate sheeting as ersatz skylights ... colour, curves and façade gimmickry are used as a guarantee of market acceptance, just as people know what to expect from a McDonalds or a Pizza Hut and feel safe about it. I would like to think that DHC can stand aside from this junk architecture. There is, or there ought to be, an intellectual component to our work, something which shows our peers and our clients that architecture is a conscious act which has a real meaning. It is more important that we have this quality than that our work exhibits all the fashionable tricks of lesser minds.

Ideally, we should have our own 'house style' of thinking and working, producing many different buildings, each the best solution in its context. This does not spell the death of fun in architecture', I said, 'but it does mean the end of hackneyed idioms and our work will be all the better for that.'

Towards the end of my first year back in town, I took a phone call from Greg Deas, who headed up the architecture division at the National Capital Development Commission, just down the road from the Department. From the time of my arrival in Canberra, I had been contacted by many architects outside the Department, some of whom I knew well and some less well and I was not surprised to get a call from Deas. His paths and mine had never really crossed, but he suggested I drop down to see him and I said I would be pleased to do this. When we met, he said he had heard I was giving directions to my architects about design and that I had banned barrel vaults, split gables, trellises, pale pink and green paint and all sorts of other decorations. He said, 'You can't do that', to which I replied, 'as a matter of fact I can'. You'll restrict the talents of your designers, he told me. No, I won't, I said, but I want the Commonwealth to get the best buildings it can afford. The Commission was at the time encouraging flirtations with postmodernism with Denton Corker Marshall's Barton cafeteria and Lawrence Nield's Caroline Chisholm School in Tuggeranong. I told Deas I did not want to see the architects in my Department outdoing each other in the pursuit of valueless fashions and I reminded him of Philip Cox's warning that 'isms' sooner or later became 'wasms'. Had Deas known it at the time, the all-powerful Commission had less than three years to live before it would be closed down forever. Had I but known it, the idea of frank and fearless advice from government architects and engineers would be jettisoned at the same time.

My choreographed visits over the first few months to the regional offices of the Department reminded me of the time when my brother and I had been herded from classroom to classroom at Telopea Park School, just ten years old and fresh from England. Tony and I were of passing interest on account of our funny little caps and our accents and we recited poems so that everyone could marvel at the way we spoke. Shuffled now among the offices of the Department in each of the States, I explained where I had come from and where I thought we

*cartoon from Queensland Region 1986*

should be going. I listened to hundreds of voices with years of professional and bureaucratic experience and tried to absorb at least some of the advice so freely given. One of the project managers said all I really needed to remember was to allow enough in the budgets for trees, because our clients didn't really want to see the buildings we gave them anyway.

When visiting the regional offices, meetings were scheduled with directors and senior staff, but I asked also to meet less formally with architectural staff, from whom I usually received a slightly different report about how things were going. Preparations for my first visit to the Queensland regional office, which was headed up by a particularly unpopular director, brought the delivery of a glorious unsigned cartoon in which I perched above it all (smoking my pipe) as part of a heavenly ruling class while the proletariat toiled away on drawing boards below a smothering raincloud. For my first visit to Darwin, John Statton helped me find shirts and shorts of the correct khaki colour. We were confident the outfit would have me taken as a local but the disguise was a failure, several Territorians telling me I obviously came from a place where men wore long trousers all the time because I had no hair on my knees.

I had brought back to Canberra an abiding interest in building materials and an antipathy to what I called lazy architecture. It was important, I told architects in the regional offices, to separate government buildings from the mass of poorly designed commercial structures around us. Look at the Street Called Straight in Damascus, I said, and then tell me you can do something as good on a military base with such simple materials. Barrel vaults were much in fashion at that time for shopping centres and fresh food markets, but I explained that the government did not build shops and there were other ways to cover large floor areas. Polycarbonate, I said, was OK for airplane windows but not much else. Cleaners were using steel wool to clean acrylic roof lights and the scratches were there forever. Teenagers had discovered they could burn nice big holes in polycarbonate with a Bic lighter and bus shelters all over Australia were now beyond repair. Careful design and construction was under threat everywhere, I said. I did not want my departmental architects to participate in the last rites of modern architecture.

I was able to visit my children Emma, Isobel and Adam in Sydney from time to time and I brought them to Canberra whenever I could. In my second year, Emma enrolled at the Canberra College of Advanced Education and she lived with me in Barton for several months. Soon after my return to Canberra, I met up again with Annabelle Rodowicz, then Annabelle Bicevskis, who had been in her final year of studies at Sydney when I went there as a lecturer in 1974. Annabelle moved to Canberra in 1980 and had worked at the NCDC and in private practice. She was now a lecturer in the School of Environmental Design at the CCAE, which became the University of Canberra in 1990.

Annabelle was deeply involved at the time with the ACT Chapter of the Institute and was coordinating professional workshops with Mads Gaardboe and Colin Stewart. She asked if I would help her with a hypothetical public program on urban design, which I was pleased to do. Not long afterwards, and not knowing any other women in Canberra, I asked her to return the favour by coming with me to a mid-winter ball organised by the Department's social club. There she met with Tony and Faith Blunn and her special friendship with them began that evening. Faith remains a close friend and Tony became one of Annabelle's mentors. I was made welcome by Annabelle's mother in Canberra and her family in Sydney and I enjoyed the company of the friends she had made in Canberra such as Jenny Tange and Gai Williamson. We were especially close to Mads Gaardboe and his wife Sue. Annabelle had worked with Mads at the NCDC and CCAE and we are the godparents of their first son Martin, now an architect in Copenhagen. Annabelle was a lot of fun to be with and we spent as much time as possible together. I liked her children Elisabeth and Luke from our very first meeting. My children got on well with Annabelle and her children and thus began an enjoyable professional association and, more importantly, an enduring romance.

*Credit where credit is due*

I developed a fondness for architects of all ages in each of the regional drawing offices and I enjoyed their presentations of current projects and the ensuing analysis and debate. There was generally a good turnout for roundtable discussions and I listened carefully to ideas and opinions about all sorts of things. I told them my concerns were with social responsibility and the historical legacy of a skilled and committed federal design group, and I said that architecture should be worthwhile fun. I wanted to help improve standards, recognise good work and learn from our mistakes. Architecture, I said, must work well and allow for change over time; we should be wary of fashion and always aim for excellence. We spoke of Mies van der Rohe and his dictum that God is in the details. We were in agreement that a sound concept deserves careful and creative detailing to bring it to a reality and that we must always do this. It is just not good enough, I said, if all that happens when you get near a building is that it gets bigger. I reminded them of the search by Robin Boyd in his 1967 Boyer lectures for a modern Australian architecture which would satisfy John Ruskin's hope for buildings that 'act well, speak well and look well' and I did my best to offer support, encouragement and peer recognition. I asked if there were any good writers among them, saying that if they were to write something

worthwhile, then I would see that it got published. I was able to say that I was working with the Institute of Architects to bring out a book devoted to the work of government architects in which they would get appropriate credit for the buildings they had done over the years.

Government architects have opportunities to work on an amazing range of projects, far more varied and challenging than they could expect even in the largest multi-disciplinary private practice. The completed works are often of the highest standard, winning government and community recognition and national and regional awards for architecture and urban design, landscape design, technology and engineering. Large commercial buildings such as the Campbell Park Offices in Canberra and the Commonwealth State Law Courts in Sydney resolve complex functional requirements with imagination and style. Military installations in all States including army and naval bases and airfields demand exceptional skills to meet operational and technological demands in sensitive environments and remote areas.

A major recent achievement for the Department had been the design and construction of the Australian Defence Force Academy in Canberra, which received numerous design prizes including the Canberra Medallion and the Sir Zelman Cowen Award, the highest awards of the Institute of Architects. The Academy offered courses in conjunction with the University of New South Wales and took over the educational streams offered previously by the RAAF Officer School at Point Cook in Victoria, the RAN Officer School at Jervis Bay and the Royal Military College at Duntroon. It aimed to be 'both Sparta and Athens', creating a physical environment that reconciled the often-conflicting theories of the military and academia. Other unusual projects in the Department, smaller in scale but equally fascinating, included prefabricated buildings at Australia's Mawson, Davis and Casey stations in Antarctica; the National Institute of Dramatic Art at the University of New South Wales; the South Australian Garden of Remembrance for the Office of Australian War Graves; dedicated heritage restorations in all parts of the country and ongoing work at several diplomatic missions overseas. I remind myself still of the remarkable catalogue of design achievements by the Department

*Campbell Park Offices*
*Canberra ACT*
*Department of Works ACT*
*Region 1977*
*James Maccormick,*
*Theo Hirsch, Max Barham,*
*Bill Adamson*
Max Dupain

and its thousands of committed professionals. I am grateful to have been involved in a small part of its story and pleased that I was able to arrange publication of a book describing in words and pictures some of this work over a period of more than seventy years.

In between interstate trips, I was busy with industry breakfasts and presentations at the CCAE and at the Canberra Institute of Technology. I found some time for writing and a second volume of *Details in Australian Architecture* was published by the Institute of Architects in 1987, which included a number of projects by the Department. In conjunction with Peter Bycroft, a senior architect in our head office, I wrote a chapter on post-occupancy evaluation entitled 'Quality Down Under' for Wolfgang Preiser's book *Building Evaluation*, which was published in New York in 1990. I accepted a small number of invitations to speak at special events, notably at a dinner at the Sydney Opera House in October 1988 to mark the fiftieth anniversary of Hassell Architects, one of Australia's largest practices, where my brother Tony had been a director for a number of years.

My attendance was required every Monday morning at a senior officers meeting called SOM (aka silly old men, there being no senior women). This exposed me from the start to the language and argot of the federal bureaucracy. I started to write down some of the things that were said at these and other meetings. Paris Drake-Brockman, one of our most urbane senior executives, said famously of a well-known person in another government department that 'she has always confused activity with achievement' and of another that 'he manages to do a second-rate job with first-rate people'. Someone in another department had been given a prize for clear writing, at which another SOM remarked that this was no way to get on in the public service. When a junior officer was reprimanded for tautology, his supervisor reported that 'initially this made no immediate difference to his writing in the first instance'.

Inspired by these literary gems, I spent winter evenings devising a board game called, of course, BUREAUCRACY. 'The object of the game', I told future participants, 'is to move through the bureaucracy and collect as many staff as possible. In the process you will also be given files that you must try to get rid of. When you enter the game, you are

*National Institue of Dramatic Art Department of Works NSW Region 1988 Peter Armstrong*

given a desk, two files and a policy card. At the first level of the game you try to get yourself a window and a computer and you must also earn a degree. When you have these and at least ten staff you can move to the second level of the bureaucracy. Here your growing importance demands that you collect around you a secretary, an executive officer and a personal assistant. With all these signs of your status and at least twenty staff you can enter the top level of the game. To win the game of bureaucracy you must have an expense account and you will of course have had an overseas trip. At this point and with at least thirty staff you declare yourself the winner. You give all your files to the players who most annoyed you on the way up and throw a large party.' I drew up a classy looking Monopoly-type board with dice and pieces shaped like armchairs with the various levels of self-importance in circles of increasing size. My friend Michael de Kretser showed my mock-up to Milton Bradley in Singapore and they expressed interest in marketing the game but nothing further came of it.

My involvement with the Institute of Architects continued at a range of scales with participation in the ACT Chapter winter speaker's series and as a member of the Chapter design awards jury. I also chaired the awards jury for the Northern Territory Chapter but was practically run out of town when I gave their top award to a humble newspaper building rather than to a large air-conditioned office block from the big end of Darwin. At the invitation of the National President of the Institute, I was a member of the national awards jury for two years and I was able to arrange my visits to the regional offices of the Department to include inspections of projects I might otherwise not have been able to see. Locally, I chaired the jury for the inaugural Marion Mahony Griffin Prize for measured drawings of heritage places, ran a competition for affordable housing and one for urban design on the west basin of the lake at Acton and gave an illustrated talk on typologies for railway stations in a competition for the design of a Very Fast Train terminal at Canberra Airport, a project initiated by Annabelle with Murray Northrop at the then CCAE.

New challenges in my second and third years back in Canberra exposed me to wider issues of performance standards and project delivery. It is not a function of government, I believe, to compete with the private sector for the delivery of goods and services but neither should governments be dictated to by commercial interests. I raised concerns about a populist view developing at the time within the federal public service that in matters of building economics we should be following commercial real estate practices. Across the Tasman, New Zealand had created a new market-led economy referred to frequently as Rogernomics (after Finance Minister Roger Douglas). Australian government departments seemed ready to accept what I saw as dangerous standards for leased properties. Real estate magicians were telling our client departments that the government had no business building or owning properties but should just rent the space it needed in the open market.

# ANNUAL EVENING SERIES. APRIL-MAY 1988, RAIA ACT CHAPTER

## INVITATION

AS A SEQUEL TO PREVIOUS YEAR'S ACCLAIMED SERIES OF TALKS BY ARCHITECTS, THE FUNCTIONS COMMITTEE (ACT CHAPTER) OF THE ROYAL AUSTRALIAN INSTITUTE OF ARCHITECTS INVITES YOU TO JOIN THEM FOR TALKS, WINE AND CHEESE AT THE PARLIAMENT HOUSE EXHIBITION CENTRE ON THE FOLLOWING FOUR EVENINGS AT 6PM

APRIL 11 — **ROGER PEGRUM**

**GREGORY BURGESS** — APRIL 18

APRIL 26 — **HARRY SEIDLER**

**RICHARD JOHNSON** — MAY 2

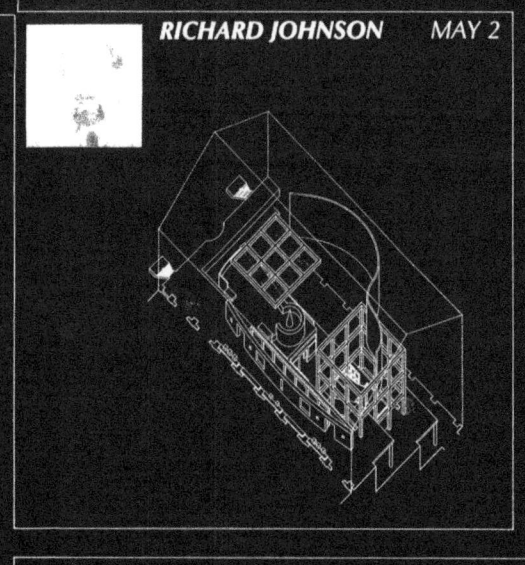

WE WOULD LIKE TO TAKE THIS OPPORTUNITY TO THANK OUR GUEST SPEAKERS AND TRUST THAT THIS SERIES WILL CONTINUE TO STIMULATE ARCHITECTURAL DISCOURSE IN THE ACT

THE SERIES IS PROUDLY SPONSORED BY: THE NATIONAL CAPITAL DEVELOPMENT COMMISSION, MUNNS SLY & PARTNERS PTY LTD, BUNNING & MADDEN, WOODS BAGOT

**ADMISSION:**     **NON-MEMBERS: $4.00**     **R.A.I.A. MEMBERS: FREE**
**ENQUIRIES: BARBARA MILLIGAN (062) 732929**

DESIGN: TOMASZ CIOLEK

I was soon drawn into a dispute with senior property officers from other agencies about, of all things, ceiling heights in workplaces. For many years, 2700 mm (9 feet in old speak) had been accepted as the minimum height for ceilings in office buildings. Suddenly there were high rise buildings offered for lease in the centre of Sydney and Melbourne with ceilings at 2400 mm. I thought my concerns were reasonable—low ceilings, particularly in large open plan offices, would not contribute to pleasant or healthy working environments and would moreover limit capacity to respond to unforeseen changes in work patterns, lighting levels or climate control or whatever. I was somewhat prescient here. Computers, then in their infancy, would soon demand new approaches to cable management with larger service risers, accessible computer floors in some areas and air conditioning upgrades to handle the heat load of a terminal on every desk. This is not easy to do if you already have ceilings at a minimum height. I said that government agencies who did not seek independent advice in property matters would be easy meat for unscrupulous developers.

This was not a fight I wanted, nor one I could win, and I was pleased to leave the battle to those with nothing better to do. I concentrated instead on something I could complete before my term in office was over, a book cataloguing some of the design achievements of the Department and its consultants, with acknowledgement of the individual architects, landscape architects, engineers and cost planners who had made it all happen. It was not certain at the start that I would find support for such a project. Governments have historically favoured a 'non-hero' philosophy where work is spoken about only as the product of a team. Public or professional recognition or (heaven forbid) individual or group authorship or acclamation is generally neither sought nor welcomed. In most areas of public life and public works this framework remains today, micro-managed by politicians or others to tell the story they would like everyone to hear. It was always thus—in my time with the government I had difficulty getting any of my three ministers to open a new facility that was not bright and cheerful and well within their electorates. In the wider world, architects in private practice are routinely recognised through design awards and articles and reviews in professional journals. By all means, retain authorship and

copyright for the Commonwealth, I said, but at the same time let us give credit to the many people who produced the work. Every architect keeps a list of his or her projects over time; to be able to say 'I worked on that' is a just reward in a profession where dedication and ridiculous working hours are taken for granted by almost everyone.

1988 was Australia's Bicentennial Year and the last year of my contract at what was by then known as Australian Construction Services within a new Department of Administrative Services. The Department of Housing and Construction had ceased to exist and Tony Blunn had moved on to the Department of the Arts, Sport, the Environment, Tourism and Territories. My new boss was Harvey Jacka, who lived in a house I had designed fifteen years before in Weston Creek. Considering the ferment of corporate change in the air, we got on very well and respected each other's points of view and expectations. When I left in December 1988, Harvey noted that I had joined the Department in 'somewhat strained and difficult circumstances following the unexpected withdrawal of your predecessor' and he thanked me generously for establishing myself quickly and creating a 'vibrancy which engendered enthusiasm among our architectural staff'. There was a busy schedule of meetings and papers to discuss the future and our regular workload continued with a full program of client meetings and submissions to the Public Works Committee. The new Parliament House would be opened by Queen Elizabeth II on 9 May 1988, following in the footsteps of her father, who had opened the first sitting of the federal parliament in Canberra on the same day in 1927. There was work to be done with the Official Establishments Trust on renovations at Government House Yarralumla for the Queen's stay and I met regularly with the NCDC to discuss how we could best contribute to all this bicentennial celebration. It was going to be a hectic year and it would also see the publication of *Australian Government Architects*, the last book in the Institute's Australian Architects series.

*Australian Government Architects* was published as an official bicentennial project of the Institute of Architects in association with the Australian Government

# AUSTRALIAN ARCHITECTS

*Australian Government Architects*

Publishing Service and was launched in November 1988 at the new Parliament House by Hon Stewart West, Minister for Administrative Services. The Institute noted that it was appropriate in the bicentennial year for an issue of their Australian Architects series to contain 'not the work of an individual architect or practice but the work of the many Australian architects who have collectively and individually contributed to the office of the Australian Government Architect':

> From the point of view of the architectural profession, such agencies provide training in the design and documentation of a range of building types not otherwise available to younger architects. These agencies provide access to those projects instilled in the higher conscience of the profession as its reason for being. Public buildings are regarded in all countries as the highlights of an architectural career. Government agencies serve often as enlightened patrons of architecture and as arbiters of architectural standards and taste. They foster promising emerging practices with the challenge of unusual projects. The people of Australia owe its Commonwealth and other government architects a great deal, directly and indirectly, both for the functional amenity of much of their physical environment and for its human and aesthetic quality.

In a foreword (which I drafted), the Minister said our book paid a 'fitting tribute to the talented and committed professional and technical officers of Australian Construction Services for their outstanding contribution over many years to Australian government architecture ... a commitment extended to many overseas countries where an Australian presence has needed to be established'. In the context of a central Commonwealth design agency, said the Minister, the book demonstrated the ability to 'rise to the occasion' and to adapt to change to suit the needs of government. The Minister concluded that a 'central Commonwealth design agency committed to fostering high professional standards is one way to ensure that the quality of work shown in this publication continues to be available throughout Australia'. With hindsight, of course, this was all nonsense. In my innocent introduction, I said the projects in the book 'show a commitment to excellence in architecture which is, and will continue to be, the major aim of all government architects'.

But the Government had already decided to do away with us all. The Commonwealth agency that began its life in 1916 as a humble branch of an infant Department of Works and Railways but had achieved so much was gone by the end of the year.

I asked Neville Quarry and Roger Johnson, two of Australia's most highly respected academics and architectural critics, to write some words about the role of government architects. Neville started his introductory essay with the paradox of unlikely praises—'one does not expect to find among the general public a consensus that public servants are creative people ... notions of imaginative action and deliberative responsibility are not seen as automatically integrated ... the daily press nurtures the view that somehow aesthetic vitality and fiscal reliability are opposed'. He suggested that the broadcasting of such ideas is the work of those 'in whom neither unique creativity nor common sensibility is evident ... architecture produced by the Commonwealth government can be and often is important, significant, valuable, cost effective, client responsive, publicly appreciated and highly regarded by the architectural profession in Australia'.

Neville noted that the design of facilities for the armed services in particular provided architects with unusual challenges and unpredictable resolutions. He found further paradoxes in the geometric order and scientific disciplines of weaponry and the apparently accidental arrangements of blast deflectors at the Tindal airfield in the Northern Territory. At Sydney's Garden Island, he said, 'government architects have restored old sheds and colonial stores and inserted hi-tech buildings for the overhaul of guided missile launching systems. There are buildings for scientific research in all parts of the country, for the protection of the natural environment and for the training of actors and film makers—a rich collection of opportunities and quality solutions. While not all these buildings are rewarded with major architectural or urban design accolades, they are at least equal to most of the buildings of the private sector'.

In a closing commentary headed 'Care and Consideration', Roger Johnson reminded us that a large number of Australian architects had acquired a good grounding of professional practice in 'the Department' before feeling able to branch out on their own. Many architects, he thought, entered the

Department as graduates or cadets as the 'young Turks' of the time, they generated a head of steam and enthusiasm, often giving quantum leaps to the standard of architecture being produced at that moment. He said some kind things about my short stay and the tenures of my predecessors Peter Hall and Bruce Bowden, commending the encouragement and acknowledgement we had given to each and all members of the team working on any project. He spoke well of the ambition for a 'house style' in our work, identifying a common thread in the 'careful placement of buildings on the site, a considered massing and articulation of buildings and a concern for maintenance-free detailing'.

Roger also hit on the special working environment of a government architectural office with his observation that 'the very nature of departmental organisation militates against exercises in individualism' which may not survive the many committees of review: 'government architecture may be strong, vital, commodious and delightful but it will rarely be overly idiosyncratic or whimsical'. He singled out some heritage and defence projects as equal to the best in the country. He noted that the Department had lived through a short 'heroic' stage of concrete brutalism, but he was not able so easily to forgive a small number of 'tricky' postmodern outcomes which he felt did not belong in the proud history of government architecture. He ended on a positive note, however, making special mention of the work of departmental architects at international expositions, starting with James Maccormick and Richard Johnson and followed by others equally skilled. Australian government architects, he thought, had maintained a consistently high standard in many areas over a long period of time. There was much to be said, he concluded, for the retention of a body of Commonwealth architects, 'if for no other reason than that professionals are best briefed by professionals ... government architects have proved that they can produce work that is equal to the best produced by the private sector'.

Bicentennial fever might have explained the lack of thought given earlier to the future of the provisional Parliament House in Canberra once the politicians and staffers had moved up to Capital Hill. Giurgola's designs for the permanent Parliament House retained the provisional building and its landscape setting as part of the overall composition of the land axis but there were inevitably those who wanted all the old stuff out of the way. Commonsense would prevail to counter these pressures but questions remained about the future use of the old building. We were asked to contribute to the debates and I proposed an informal meeting of folk likely to have strong ideas on a future role for the building and grounds. In April 1988, we hired a nice big room at the back of the newly refurbished Hyatt Canberra Hotel with a view of the sunny gardens and I arranged for comfortable chairs and continuous coffee and cakes to consider these small but important things.

I assembled my panel with some care, starting with two locals, Manning Clark and Fred Daly. Manning Clark, arguably Australia's most important historian, had lived with his family since 1953 in a house designed by Robin Boyd in Tasmania Circle Forrest and it was there that he had written his six volumes of *A History of Australia*. We were all aware of his friendship with Romaldo Giurgola and their regular meetings on a simple bench seat at the end of the Lawns at Manuka. Manning accepted willingly my invitation to participate in a one-day talkfest. Fred Daly, who had launched *The Bush Capital* in 1983, was a charming raconteur with a vast knowledge of the workings of the Parliament. He had been a minister in the Whitlam government and had sat in the House of Representatives in the old building for more than thirty years. Widely referred to as the 'King of Canberra', Daly and his Old English sheepdog (named Sir John after you know who) were popular members of the Canberra community.

My other panel members were equally impressive. Peter Spearritt was a respected historian at Macquarie University whose book *The Open Air Museum* I had reviewed a few years earlier for the ABC. He was well known for his opinion that Australia did not at that time take the twentieth century seriously but he was at the same time personally unimpressed with the new Parliament building, which he described as 'four-fifths office block'. I was pleased also to get Gavin Souter to Canberra for the day. Souter was widely regarded as an authority on the defining moments of federation and his book *Lion and Kangaroo* is an engrossing account of the first years of the Commonwealth. Present also for the day at our invitation were representatives from the National Capital Development Commission and Australian Archives. The National Library recorded the proceedings and have retained a transcript for their records. I also commissioned Ian Warden, a journalist with *The Canberra Times*, to prepare a commentary on the forum for more immediate consideration by the various stakeholders.

Warden described us at the start of the day as a 'panel of thinkers and dreamers and pragmatists sitting down with a model of the old building in front of us like surgeons discussing what to do with a patient etherised upon the table'. Fred Daly spoke first to remind us that the building had not always been comfortable. Manning Clark noted that sensitive visitors to the Australian War Memorial weep, but Gavin Souter thought that visitors to the old House after it was emptied might instead yawn. Peter Spearritt thought Australians might be fond of the building because, unlike the forbidding High Court, it was 'cute and approachable', blessed with both human scale and dignity. Michael Grace of the National Capital Development Commission suggested that, as we approached the end of the twentieth century, the whole parliamentary zone might gain 'a greater mystique and national reverence' as a sort of 'heart of the nation'.

*Australian pavilion*
*International Exposition*
*Osaka Japan 1970*
*Department of Works*
*ACT Region*
*James Maccormick,*
*Theo Hirsch, Max Barham*
National Archives

Manning Clark was not surprisingly committed to Australians knowing more about themselves. The building must not, he said, degenerate into a series of meaningless displays and there should be a theme about the enormous changes since the opening of the building in 1927, from 'being part of the Empire to being grown up'. Gavin Souter thought the place ought to be a 'museum of Australian identity' covering far more than parliamentary politics. Fred Daly saw the old Cabinet room as especially sacred, a place where crucial things were decided in what he called 'some very grim days'. There was discussion as to whether Australians shared the 'intellectual tradition' of Americans and whether there was any point in preserving chairs or other objects 'once graced by statesmanlike bottoms'. The role of the press was recognised late in the day, and it was agreed by everyone present that the fourth estate deserved to be incorporated into the general environment as it had been when the House was their place of work. It was generally accepted that some space in a sunny corner of the building should be set aside for the use of historians or political scientists and everybody agreed that charging for entry to the building would be 'bizarre' when admission to the new Parliament House would be free.

At the end of the day, Harvey Jacka thanked the participants for their time and energy. Their discussions and ideas, he assured us, would feed into a submission to Cabinet as part of a process to legitimise the commonly accepted belief that the old building would have a value in years to come. In 1997, I was appointed as a foundation member of the Governing Council of Old Parliament House and took part for some years in the first steps in its new life, which included providing the first home for the National Portrait Gallery. This seemed a fitting finale to my relationship with a building I had known for almost fifty years.

# Selling Dreams

*General Post Office Adelaide. Architects Wright and Wood 1872. Conservation by Department of Works SA/NT region 1986. Colin Schumacher/Robert Dusting in association with Danvers Architects*

Annabelle and I were married at the end of January 1988 and we took Elisabeth and Luke with us on a short honeymoon to the South Coast. Because it was the bicentennial year, somebody stuck a funny little green stamp in the shape of Australia (but of course without Tasmania) on our marriage certificate, just like the stickers you now find on apples or mangoes. Annabelle had been in Canberra for almost ten years and we decided that was where we belonged. I thanked Sydney University for keeping my position open but said I would not be coming back. We bought an Oakley and Parkes cottage in Melbourne Avenue with a pleasant garden. We added some living space and restored its fireplaces and internal timber details and lived there happily for nearly twenty years.

Annabelle's career has taken a different path from mine but our commitment to Canberra is a shared passion. She graduated from the University of Sydney with first class honours and the Leslie Wilkinson Prize for design history and theory and joined the new ACT public service in 1990, moving from traditional areas to various senior roles including ACT Chief Planner and Executive Director of the Cabinet and Policy Office. In 1998 she was the Telstra ACT Business Woman of the Year and not long after took up the post of Chief Executive at the National Capital Authority, a position she held for almost ten years. In 2007, she was appointed as a Member in the Order of Australia for service to architecture and to the planning, promotion, enhancement and development of Australia's national capital. Our interests in architecture and in Canberra have been expressed in many rewarding ways and we have supported one another personally and professionally. We are also fortunate to be blessed with fine friends and wonderful children and grandchildren.

Throughout 1988 I said no to various offers to stay on and assist with the privatisation of public works for a government I saw as blinded by economic rationalism. In 1989, I joined the established architectural practice of Jackson Teece Chesterton Willis as a partner in their Canberra office, which was managed at the time by Bruce Fisher. Jackson Teece had come to Canberra some years before to build a new office building for the Attorney-General's Department on Kings Avenue and a bus depot at Tuggeranong. David Jackson was the President of the Institute of Architects when I came back to Canberra and he had chaired the Institute's national awards jury in 1986 and 1987. I had known Angus Teece during my time in Sydney, when we each had children at Woollahra Demonstration School. I respected his architectural judgment and we were good if not close friends. Michael Bennett, an architect and gifted artist, was a director in their head office in Sydney and I admired his skills and was grateful for his friendship. Their office had a low profile in Canberra and I told anyone who asked at the time that my aim was to make it one of the top three practices in town. Also working in our small Deakin office was Tomasz Ciolek, a talented architect and delineator with whom I formed a personal friendship and a creative professional association over the next several years. My time with Jackson Teece was productive and always interesting but it did not end well.

By 1989 the population of Canberra was almost 300 000, a far cry from the 25 000 expected at the turning of the first sod seventy-five years before. In late April, the ACT Chapter of the Institute of Architects hosted the Institute's national convention in Canberra with the theme *Private Spaces and Public Places*. It was a good time for architects to gather in the national capital. Romaldo Giurgola's bold new Parliament House was finished and open for peer review. Lots of other bicentennial projects were on show

*Calthorpes' House, Red Hill ACT architect Ken Oliphant conservation Department of Works 1986 ACT Region Richard Ratcliffe in association with Philip Cox and Partners*

including Lawrence Nield's National Science and Technology Centre; the shiny new buildings of the Australian Institute of Sport by Phillip Cox and Daryl Jackson and the glories of W Hayward Morris's 1930s Institute of Anatomy, now reborn as the National Film and Sound Archive. The month before, the citizens of the Australian Capital Territory had elected their first-ever local government. Many in the community dreaded the prospect of local politics and feared for the future of the city. The good burghers showed their displeasure with the whole political process by putting up a vast array of would-be legislators and protest groups like the Sun Ripened Warm Tomato Party and the Party Party Party. Not content with sweeping away the last remnants of the Department of Works, the Commonwealth also dismantled the National Capital Development Commission. Responsibility for

*Reserve Bank Staff Training College 1988 Kirribilli Department of Works NSW Region in association with Allen Jack and Cottier.*

the national areas of the city was handed over to a new National Capital Planning Authority, later re-named the National Capital Authority, and planning for the rest of the town would be controlled by an as yet unnamed agency of the Territory Government. It was a confusing time indeed in the bush capital.

Registrations for the Institute convention dramatically exceeded expectations. Annabelle and I were involved in much of the pre-planning, but the driving force was local architect Neil Renfree, whose organisational abilities made it a runaway financial success as well as an informative and creative event. The convention program was full and challenging and delegates received good value for their registration fee. A student conference was run concurrently with the main program, and the students had fun at a two-day workshop to design an official residence for the new ACT Chief Minister somewhere on the lakeshore but not too close to the territorians she would be governing.

The venue for the convention was the recently upgraded Hyatt Hotel on Commonwealth Avenue. The Albert Hall next door was used for plenary sessions and exhibitions and was the setting for an entertaining student cabaret. Annabelle and I had been in Ottawa the year before, where we met Canadian architect Douglas Cardinal at his new Museum of Civilisation. Of Native Canadian heritage, Cardinal was known for his smooth and flowing building forms and he later designed the National Museum of the American Indian on the Mall in Washington DC. At our invitation, Cardinal agreed to travel to Canberra and he was the keynote speaker on the opening day. Cardinal spoke of tradition and identity in architecture, important themes in many capital cities at that time, and the pivotal role of the architect in making places private or public or maybe both. He was followed by Los Angeles architect Michael Pittas, a member of the Washington Fine Arts Commission, who discussed the roles of both government and private enterprise in the creation of quality urban environments. There was also an excellent presentation on the first day by Australian architect David Allen, then living in London, whose work in providing decent infrastructure for squatter communities in middle eastern countries had earned him international recognition. Almost thirty years later, these concerns remain relevant to architects and urban planners. We are still to make meaningful inroads into place making and the provision of affordable housing.

The second day of the convention was Anzac Day and visiting delegates joined locals for the dawn service at the Australian War Memorial. Later that afternoon, awards were presented for a national urban design competition sponsored by the new National Capital Planning Authority and the equally new ACT Administration. The competition sought ideas for the revitalisation of Civic Centre and the area around City Hill, the third corner of Walter Burley Griffin's great national triangle. Architects know that design competitions challenge their ideas and test their skills in communication. In talks to students over many years, I have described this aspect of architecture as 'selling dreams'. Over the next two years, Tomasz Ciolek and I won first prizes in two urban design competitions, one for Canberra and one in Sydney, followed by a win in an invited competition for a major new faculty building at the University of Sydney.

*The City Hill Urban Design Competition*

For the City Hill competition, Tomasz and I spent a large number of evening and weekend hours preparing our submission with the assistance of Fred Kasparek, a young architect in the Deakin office. The competition had a first prize of $4000 and attracted a respectable total of 39 entries. All of the submissions were mounted on boards and displayed in the Palm Court at the Hyatt Hotel prior to the announcement of the winners. My heart sank a little when I saw that our design had been given the notional number 29. This was the date of my birthday, but 29 was also the number that had been given to Walter Burley Griffin's entry in the 1912 competition for the design of Australia's capital city. I hoped this was a good omen and when we were announced as the winners we were of course delighted. Second prize went to Mark Willett, Katherine Lakis and Dilip Patel of the MSJ Group and third prize to Daniel Jang Jong with Phillipa McMahon.

The jury for the competition was chaired by Michael Pittas and included Douglas Cardinal, Romaldo Giurgola and the New South Wales Government Architect Andrew Andersons. The results of the competition were published widely and there was positive public comment for the way in which our submission offered solutions to problems like the isolation of City Hill and the division of the city into two by Northbourne Avenue. There was also support for our inclusion of the 'missing link' from Commonwealth Park to City Hill with a land bridge across Parkes Way. We diverted traffic around City Hill along Marcus Clarke Street, a simple but effective solution that was killed stone dead almost immediately by powerful retail and commercial interests. The jury said it was impressed with our 'rich composition' and 'scope of invention' and by the 'dramatised level change leading up to a formal urban park' on top of City Hill. We proposed a new and much larger city square at the junction of Northbourne Avenue and London Circuit, saying that 'even if we can't afford to build it now, at least we can set the area aside and not build over it', another good idea constantly under threat from politicians and real estate developers. The *Canberra Times* published our designs and ran a full-page story, saying the competition had produced the 'sort of positive answers' that the NCDC 'could never quite come up with'.

*City Hill Competition 1989*

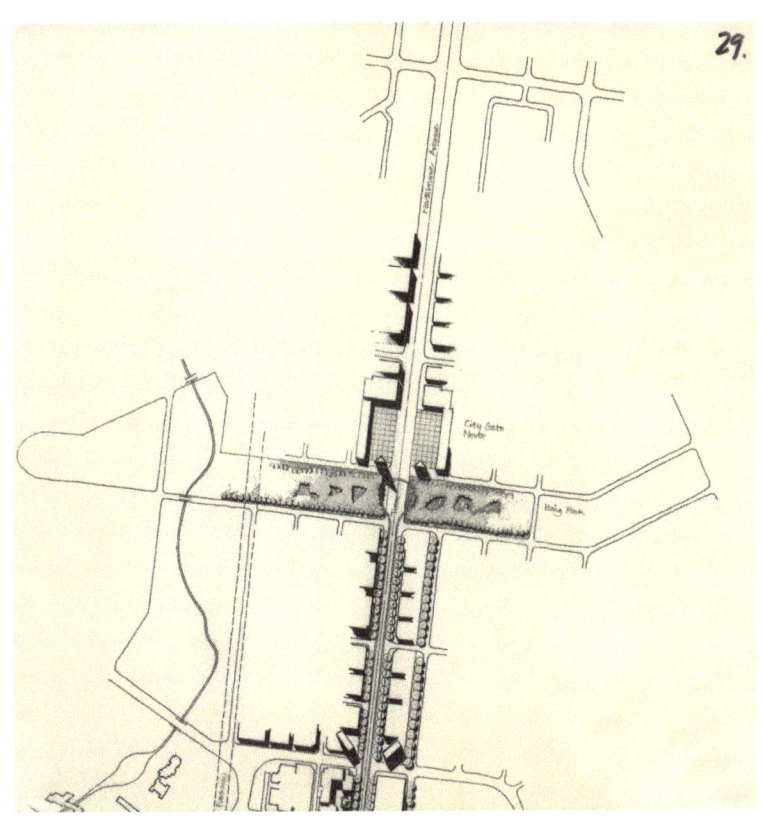

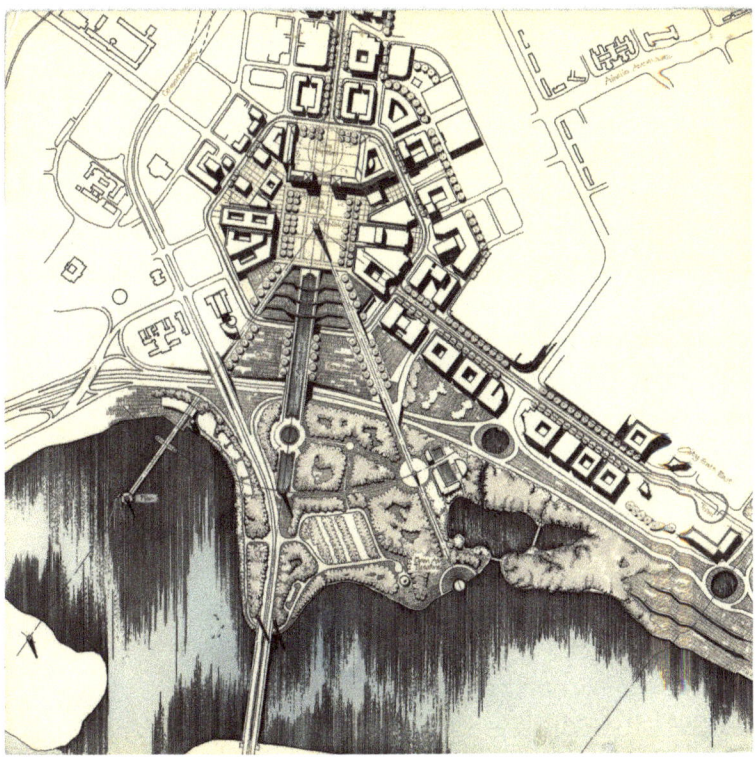

Elizabeth Farrelly wrote in *Architecture Australia* that the competition was run 'in the hope of finding a way to give Canberra the City Centre it never had'. Farrelly said our scheme would 'reinstate Northbourne Avenue as the primary, almost ceremonial, entrance to the city and restore at least visual links between the city's municipal and national precincts'. She noted the role we had given to 'city gates' at Haig Park and on the eastern approach to the city along Constitution Avenue. Farrelly concluded that the decision of the assessors was 'accurate and courageous' and rewarded the capacity to think beyond the confines of the site. Griffin's design may yet become a 'fine urban cloth', she said, and there was certainly general agreement as to 'the sensitivity with which this cloth is laid on the landscape'. Farrelly hoped there would be a centenary of federation competition which would give Griffin's design a final vote of confidence such as the City Beautiful movement had brought to L'Enfant's plans for Washington DC a century before or, failing that, a final redirection of the city dream in another direction. Either way, she said, Canberra needs that 'golden guiding vision'.

Sadly, the City Hill competition went the way of many urban design competitions, all a bit too difficult for our leaders to grasp and impossible to build within the electoral cycle. In the last 25 years, only two projects have touched on the urban design opportunities of City Hill and its immediate environs. Each of these was spawned by the publication in 2004 of *The Griffin Legacy*, a ground-breaking research project initiated by Annabelle Pegrum at the National Capital Authority, which looked at some of the unrealised ideas in Griffin's designs for Canberra to see what could sensibly be added to what had been built so far. Robert Freestone has described *The Griffin Legacy* as 'Australia's most ambitious attempt to correlate urban design needs and opportunities with historical influences'. Noting Griffin's statements that the central lakes are one of the 'most valuable features of the city plan and of the city site', the *Legacy* suggested it might be possible to 'extend the City to the Lake' and provide a 'waterfront promenade for Civic' with a generous linear foreshore park on West Basin.

The idea of extending the built form of the city towards the lake was in due course seized upon by the territory government as a 'transformational project' and touted as 'integral to realising the city's potential'. But when concept plans for the project were released, the 55 metre wide waterfront promenade proposed in the *Legacy* had become a narrow footpath plus a timber boardwalk hovering over the water. I suggested at the time that a fine grain of streets and building forms would be needed to link West Basin to the existing city pattern, saying that we must avoid forever separating the city from the lake in the way that the Kingston Foreshore development was walling off south Canberra from the water. All sections of the Canberra community await further proposals for this key site.

A second proposition of *The Griffin Legacy* was to complete Griffin's municipal main street on the bones of the neglected Constitution Avenue. The *Legacy* said this should be a modern day mixed-use and busy boulevard with broad sidewalks and sunny outdoor dining—'the elegant high street of the city ... lined with shops, cafes and a mix of commercial, entertainment and residential uses'. The roadworks have since been completed but in the manner of an arterial road rather than a city street and the narrow carriageways have been painted with all manner of arrows and instructions for cars and buses. An unnecessary run of closely-spaced trees down the middle ensures that you cannot see from one side of the street to the other and not more than a few metres along its length, quite at odds with Griffin's original hopes for an expansive prospect and a concave profile from City Hill. I must say that Annabelle disagrees with my views on Constitution Avenue. I hope I may be proven wrong one day, but I have a feeling that Constitution Avenue will never be an attractive city street until the central median is removed.

*The Sydney Showgrounds Competition*

Back in 1989, Tomasz and I were not yet finished with competitions. In November that year, we were awarded one of four first prizes in a national urban design competition for the 28-hectare site of the Sydney Showgrounds at Moore Park. Sponsored by the NSW State Government, the Royal Australian Planning Institute and the Royal Agricultural Society, the competition sought ideas for the future use of the land after a planned move by the Agricultural Society and the Royal Easter Show to the western suburbs of Sydney. The competition jury was chaired by Ken Woolley and included Andrew Andersons, Sydney architect and urban planner Tony Corkhill, heritage conservation expert James Semple Kerr and urban designer Jonathan Barnett from Baltimore, author of *The Elusive City*.

Entrants were allowed to submit up to four large drawings but we squeezed all our ideas onto a single A1 board. We called our design *The City Gardens* and promised it would give Sydney 'a first-class pleasure ground along the lines of the Tivoli Gardens in Copenhagen'. The design retained 'the several splendid buildings erected by the Royal Agricultural Society over the previous hundred years ... combined fine landscape detailing with restaurants and outdoor eating for large numbers of visitors ... the Hordern Pavilion will become a wintergarden to give year-round life to the Gardens'. The Sydney newspapers loved it. We excavated the Parade Ring and filled it with water to make a large lake, which we thought might be 'the focus for musical entertainments' but which the newspapers suggested would be more fun if used for mock (or real) naval battles. The City Gardens, we said, would offer residents and visitors a safe and attractive urban park only minutes from the centre of the city. The jury reported that our submission 'contains a powerful idea ... distinguished by its preservation of the historic buildings, the extension of a public park throughout the scheme and the maintenance of privacy and residential character linked to the neighbouring residential areas'.

In the next year, we were successful in obtaining work for the Canberra office from the ACT government and we completed small groups of garden flats in Belconnen and Tuggeranong and the refurbishment of an early Ken Woolley public housing development in Holt. We were awarded a Certificate of Merit from the ACT Chapter of the Institute of Architects for a new primary school at Gordon, in the far south of the city. Private commissions included master planning for a housing estate in Woden and designs for a roof over the Olympic Swimming Pool on Constitution Avenue. The Sydney office of Jackson Teece at this time had also done well and had won prizes in an ideas competition for the colourful but 'tired and battered' Taylor Square. The Sydney office was also selected to participate in a major competition for the site of the first Government House in Phillip Street and had formed an association for this purpose with the Washington DC office of Skidmore Owings and Merrill. The Jackson Teece/SOM submission did not win the competition but their proposal was placed second after the designs of Denton Corker Marshall.

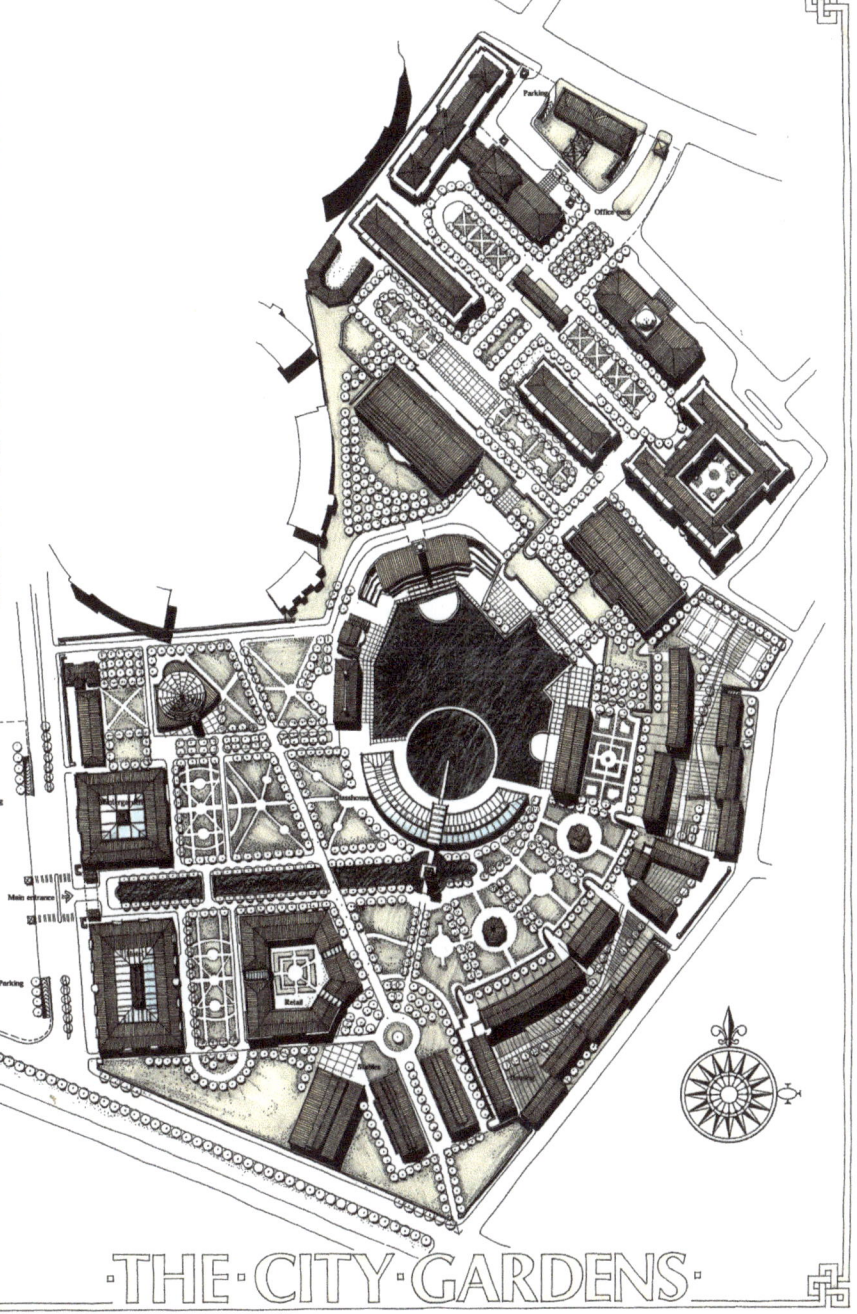

The City Gardens will give Sydney a first class pleasure ground along the lines of Tivoli Gardens in Copenhagen. The Gardens occupy half of the existing Showground site and are designed to take advantage of the several splendid buildings erected by the Royal Agricultural Society in the last 100 years. An office park is proposed for the north end of the site, integrated with the large Manufacturers' Hall and the Commemorative Pavilion, which will be converted to corporate headquarters. On the eastern edge of the site is an extensive housing development.

The Gardens will combine fine landscape detailing with restaurants and outdoor eating for large numbers of visitors. The Royal Hall of Industries will become a major hotel, with additional services and high quality retail outlets built to the east. The Hordern Pavilion will become the wintergarden to give year-round life to the Gardens.

A large lake on the Parade Ring site will be the focus for musical entertainments. The design retains the Members Grandstand, the Coronation Stand, the Suttor Stand and the RAS Council Offices, completing the arena with a new curved glasshouse and exhibition hall.

The leafy walks and terraces will bring new life to the site. The Gardens will offer residents of Sydney and visitors a safe and attractive urban park only minutes from the centre of the city. Adequate parking for cars and buses will be provided underground on the west side of Driver Avenue. Links are maintained for equestrian access to Centennial Park. It is envisaged that the Gardens and the hotel will be attractive to country visitors.

The office park has seven new buildings which make use of the level changes to respect the streetscape of Moore Park Road and to create an elegant backdrop to the Gardens. Extensive terracing on the edge of the Gardens links them visually to the office areas and the housing. Underground parking for the office buildings may also be used for sporting and other events at the Cricket Ground and the Football Stadium.

Housing along Cook Road addresses existing medium density development at the street frontage. A second layer of housing borders the Gardens in the form of medium rise apartments. Depending upon the mix of unit types, the site will accommodate between 400 and 600 units and a population up to 1800 people.

## THE · CITY · GARDENS

*The University of Sydney Competition*

In August 1991, Jackson Teece was invited to take part in two significant design competitions, one for the University of Sydney and the other at the University of Newcastle. The timetables for the two competitions overlapped and it was at first thought unlikely that the practice would be able to enter both. David Jackson decided to keep the Newcastle project for the Sydney office and offered the competition for the Faculty of Education at the University of Sydney to the Canberra office. We would be up against three heavyweight architectural practices—Mitchell/Giurgola and Thorp, Daryl Jackson Robin Dyke and Philip Cox Richardson Taylor. The site was in the northern part of the old campus, fronting the busy Manning Road and astride the long Wilkinson axis from Science Road to the picturesque Physics Building. Next door to the west was the imposing pile of the 1921 Teachers College by NSW Government Architect George McRae, delightfully described by noted historian Trevor Howells as 'Gothic Revival on a shoestring'. On the other side was the pre-World War I Women's Union at Manning House by B J Waterhouse and H V Vernon. Tomasz and I decided we would give this competition a very serious go.

I knew the precinct well from my years at the University and Tomasz and I spent many hours walking along the narrow streets and around and through the old brick and stone buildings. The hockey field behind the site had been the scene of our epic match with Pakistan thirty years earlier. Making reference to the materials and detail of the immediate surroundings and building not across but on each side of the Wilkinson line, our submission contrasted dramatically with the structuralist and uncompromising designs of our fellow competitors. An elegant model in untreated timber told the University it could have a building that would look forward and sideways at the same time. Michael Bennett prepared several delightful renderings of the building in its landscape and human setting. We were pleased with the way our building blended into the meandering pattern of Manning Road and yet maintained a strict geometry at the lower end of the site. Of the other designs submitted, only that of Mitchell/Giurgola and Thorp reflected the primacy of the Wilkinson axis and addressed the skewed alignment of Manning Road and the hockey square.

Tomasz and I thought our design stacked up well. We did not presume to think it might beat the others and my Sydney partners gave no indication that we could possibly win in such exalted company. I saw it as a seminal project for all of us and for the University but the Sydney office seemed distinctly off-hand about our chances. On Tuesday 6 November 1990, each of the four architectural offices presented their designs to the University in the lofty hall of the Merewether Building on City Road. I was on first after lunch but I was stopped abruptly about halfway through my presentation (no Powerpoint in those days, it was all done with an overhead projector and felt pens on acetate sheets) when the chairman announced a short adjournment so we could watch the running of the Melbourne Cup in the room next door. After the race that stops the nation was over (the favourite Kingston Rule won in record time at 7/1), I took up rather shakily where I had left off. A few weeks later, Jackson Teece was told it had won the competition at the University of Newcastle. Only days after that, the University of Sydney announced that we had also won the competition for their new Education Building.

On the strength of our earlier competition successes and the small but steady flow of work we were getting in Canberra, I had started an office Christmas tradition of late afternoon drinks in the garden of our house in Forrest with a small jazz band from the Canberra School of Music. The Faculty of Education was our latest and most significant triumph, a plum job by any measure and an important addition I thought to the catalogue of Jackson Teece work. The sun shone on the afternoon of our office party that year but our celebrations turned out to be premature when David Jackson took me aside to say that the Sydney directors had decided that design development and documentation for the Faculty of Education project would be transferred immediately to the Sydney office. It was a sad end to a promising episode in my professional life. For a month, Tomasz and I had been planning for the challenge of detailing our design for construction. Trevor Howells later called the building 'the University's only full-bloodied excursion into Post Modernism'. He thought it was 'curiously successful, if a little overworked',

*University of Sydney Education Building competition 1991*

but in my view a simple and promising design concept had been damaged beyond repair. The inevitable and speedy divorce from Jackson Teece was messy. Tomasz and I set up as Pegrum/Ciolek, moving to an office in Manuka in the same building as Romaldo Giurgola and working together happily and fruitfully for the next four years until Tomasz moved overseas for family reasons.

Our deep dismay at the loss of the project at the University of Sydney was softened when the new office of Pegrum/Ciolek was engaged for the design of a high school in the Tuggeranong Valley to the south of the city. We saw it as an opportunity to build a thoughtful multivalent building for a new twenty-first century generation. We were overflowing with ideas. We embraced emerging concerns for environmental responsibility and sustainability and suggested that the building might also

*Lanyon High School*

*View down Manning Road*
del M Bennett

*View to north on
Wilkinson axis*
del M Bennett

encourage community programs and evening classes such as those run at Canberra High School in the early 1950s. We suggested that the school might double as a satellite campus of the Canberra Institute of Technology, an arrangement such as Lake Ginninderra College later established with the University of Canberra. Our plans showed faculties spreading out as branches from a linear spine linked by pleasant courtyards. Each branch would have its roof water pumped up to a storage tank with a gravity feed to planter beds for staff and students. We were enjoying getting our teeth into a good-sized public building and our concept diagrams and sketches were simple and imaginative.

But Canberra's embryo public works department wanted nothing to do with any of this. 'It wouldn't look right', they said, for a government school to have half a dozen corrugated iron tanks on tall steel stands. We were told (seriously!) that the teenagers of Tuggeranong would enjoy shooting bullet holes in the tanks and probably the walls of the building at the same time. Our corridor spine had accessible ducts running the full length of the building above door head height, carrying power and communication cables to network the whole school. These perfectly sensible proposals were rejected simply because 'it had not been done before'. It was easier, we were told, to bury wires behind plasterboard in stud walls because that was how electricians had always wired buildings. Self-serving advice from a construction manager appointed without reference to us then convinced the client department to change just about everything else. We wept when the project officer told us all he really wanted was for the building to be finished on time. Only one big idea survived—lengthy swales directing all water landing on the site into a clay-lined dam. Water was pumped from the dam to irrigate the playing fields and a family of ducks took up residence almost immediately at the front door of the school. The dam and the ducks won us a major prize for environmental management, but we could not bring ourselves to nominate our ruined designs for any other award.

*The Chancery at Government House*

In November 1993, the National Capital Planning Authority, on behalf of Government House and the Official Establishments Trust, invited Pegrum/Ciolek to participate in a competition for the design of a new office building within the grounds of Government House at Yarralumla. I believe that two other Canberra practices were invited, one with a far bigger office than ours, and there was also an architect from Melbourne. We were briefed at Government House by Doug Sturkey, the Official Secretary to the Governor-General, who told us the Chancery would be a working office building for a range of vice-regal functions including meetings of the Executive Council and presentations of credentials by ambassadors and high commissioners. The Governor-General at the time was Bill Hayden, a former member of the House of Representatives, who had succeeded Gough Whitlam as leader of the Labor opposition on Whitlam's retirement in 1978. Hayden was replaced rather abruptly by Bob Hawke on the eve of the federal election in 1983, which Hawke went on to win by a large majority. Hawke's later offer to Hayden of the post of Governor-General was widely seen as an apology for denying him the chance of becoming Prime Minister of Australia.

A spacious formal office was required for the Governor-General with a smaller study for Mrs Hayden plus a conference room and offices of various sizes for personal and support staff. Also needed was a large room for the aides-de-camp, who at that time were all serving military officers. Storage space was needed for gifts from official visitors and there would be any number of issues of security and communication that must be handled with some delicacy. We took the briefing very seriously and I drew up a series of functional diagrams and concept plans which formed part of the later return brief. The site for the new building was about 100 metres to the west of the main House. There was a gentle slope to the north with a long frontage to the Lake and uninterrupted views towards Black Mountain. In the north-west corner of the site was a mature Yellow Box (eucalyptus melliodora), a significant landscape element and one of only two trees of this type in the grounds that were remnants of the original pastoral setting. The first words from Mr Hayden when we met were 'you know there's a great big tree there, don't you

Mr Pegrum ... be careful, if it dies so do you'. I thought I saw him smile, but I could not be sure of this.

The site for the Chancery was at the end of a long drive from the front gates along the western avenue. I thought the building ought to be visible from some distance away, perhaps with low hedges to create spatial definition for the roadway and to frame an arrival forecourt. To one side of the site was the original boiler house and a picturesque two-storey stables building by Goulburn architect E C Manfred dating from the early 1900s. In the south-west corner on the approach road was the oldest building in the grounds of Government House, an overseer's cottage which we would conserve and fit out as additional office space. It was a wonderful setting for an important building and we imagined the Governor-General finishing breakfast and heading off to work, no longer down the corridor in the old House but a short walk (or perhaps a longer stroll on a sunny day) through most attractive gardens.

We presented our ideas and a neat little cardboard model at Government House in the week before Christmas. The interview panel included representatives of the Trust and officers of the Planning Authority and the Department of the Prime Minister and Cabinet. Our design was crisp and modern but I told the panel that the walls would be finished in pebble dashed render to match the older buildings, and we intended to use steel framed windows to pick up the scale and finer detail of timber transoms and mullions

*Governor-General's study*

nearby. Larger areas of glass at the ground floor would give views through the building to the stables and gardens beyond. The vice-regal reception rooms at the upper level had terraces and French doors overlooking the gardens and the lake and Mrs Hayden would even have a fireplace.

There was a happy start to our new year when we took delivery of a letter from the Official Secretary: 'after weighing the presentations ... for the new office building at Government House, I have pleasure in informing you that we feel that the two-storey approach advanced by your firm conceptually comes closest to meeting our needs. I write therefore to offer you a commission to design a building which could be constructed at an all-inclusive cost not to exceed two million dollars ... if you felt able to accept this commission, we should welcome an opportunity for a discussion about it and to develop our client needs in greater detail'. Goody goody.

This would be our most challenging project to date and we loved every minute of its design andconstruction.

*Approach with Overseer's Cottage in foreground*

*View from the Lake*

It was delivered as a lump sum contract by Concrete Constructions, and everybody took very good care of Mr Hayden's great big tree. All excavation in that corner of the site was by hand and I was there with an arborist for many hours while holes were drilled between the roots. Conservation of the overseer's cottage was carried out with the assistance of Clive Lucas, one of Australia's leading heritage architects, whose work maintains the principle of doing 'as much as necessary but as little as possible'. It was good to work with Clive's site architect, Hector Abrahams, who had been a student of mine at Sydney, and the quiet presence of the restored cottage adds greatly to the character of the Chancery precinct. There were regular meetings with the Governor-General and Mrs Hayden to let them know how it was all going and to discuss details of interior finishes including timber panelling in his office and a yellowblock sandstone mantel and hearth to Mrs Hayden's fireplace. Mr Hayden was generally enthusiastic and supportive but did not much like my suggestion to use polished terrazzo for a long bench in his bathroom. 'I was a policeman once', he said, and I replied, 'yes, I know, Your

Excellency'. 'Hotels in Ipswich have terrazzo floors', he said, 'when I see terrazzo I think of piss'. Would he prefer a timber benchtop? I asked. Perhaps I could have Jarrah, he replied, and that is what he got.

Prime Minister Paul Keating opened the Chancery on a sunny winter's morning in August 1995 and said some nice things about the slender steel frame windows and how the building sat well with its older neighbours. When *The Canberra Times* was not invited to visit and photograph the new Chancery, they published a sketch by Geoff Pryor of a Yarralumla Taj Mahal and I was reminded of the Pickering cartoon twenty years earlier about my police boxes. Mr Hayden was followed as Governor-General by Sir William Deane. One of my fondest memories is of Sir William and Lady Deane strolling from the House to the Chancery hand

Mrs Hayden's study

in hand. On one occasion they arrived at the main door with their large German Shepherd dog, who raced up the main staircase in two huge bounds, skidding to a halt on a large rug. I was delighted also that Dame Quentin Bryce spoke of her pleasure at working in the Chancery building and that for the Historic Memorials Collection portrait by Ralph Heimans she elected to stand at the door from her study to the terrace.

The idea of a 'national university' in the national capital city gained currency towards the end of the Second World War. It was thought that this should be a different sort of university for a 'new and freer society in the post-war era'. The Director-General of Post-War Reconstruction, Dr H C Coombs, who would later be a Chancellor of the University, said it should be dedicated to research and postgraduate study—'a kind of intellectual powerhouse for the rebuilding of society'. But the name 'The Australian National University' was not a popular choice, thought by some to be pretentious and cumbersome and 'implying a comprehensive character and superior status which the University might not have'. Robert Menzies, who would be Prime Minister when the first buildings at the University were completed, expressed horror at the name. David Rivett, head of the Council of Commonwealth Scientific and Industrial Research, said the name was awful and that whenever he heard it he wanted to add 'Pty Ltd'.

At the heart of the University would be University House, a residential hall on the lines of an English college, designed 'on the staircase rather than the corridor principle', which would have residential accommodation for academic staff and around 100 postgraduate students plus dining and other public facilities. This 'faculty club' was expected to demonstrate 'good taste and reticence rather than extravagance' and provide an environment where 'a certain amount of gracious living would be possible'. Brian Lewis, foundation professor of architecture at the University of Melbourne, was appointed as consulting architect for University House, where he worked in association with the newly appointed

*The Australian National University*

*The Australian National
University 1954
University House
architect Brian Lewis
Sulman Medal 1954
25-Year Award 1995*
Wolfgang Sievers

*Post-graduate flat, 1960s*

University Architect John Scollay. The Commonwealth Department of Works was engaged to manage construction. Fine design, good taste and gracious living were all recognised when University House was opened by the Duke of Edinburgh in 1954 and received the Sulman Medal of the Institute of Architects, and again in 1995 when the building received the 25-Year Award for Enduring Architecture. Over the years, the role of University House has expanded to include hotel-style accommodation for non-students, with restaurants and common rooms available for hire for public events in a pleasant landscape setting.

We were engaged by the University to work with the Master of the House, Dr Rafe de Crespigny, to upgrade the accommodation and undertake essential service improvements to meet statutory requirements for public safety. University House in the 1990s was physically much as Lewis had left it and we found that the building had 'aged gracefully without the usual structural blemishes of its time'. While not at all lavish, it had the comforts sought by its founders—small private dining rooms, a porter's flat and rooms for the ladies with gardens designed by Lindsay Pryor. Construction was traditional, with loadbearing brick walls and concrete floors. The design of the rooms around a dozen individual staircases had allowed the House to be built in separate sections by different gangs of bricklayers and carpenters. This had produced endearing differences in levels and finishes in the lobbies which we were careful to keep. We took care too with the replacement of the bathroom floor heating, laying new terrazzo flooring to match the original precisely. There was great joy when we discovered a vast room over the Acton road tunnel full of Fred Ward furniture which we lovingly restored with the assistance of a small team of cabinet makers in Queanbeyan.

We prepared a conservation management plan for the building and grounds and assessed its significance against the criteria for the inclusion of places in the then Register of the National Estate. Our statement of significance noted the role played by University House

*The Hall at University House before installation of Leonard French works* Regeneration *and* Journey

*Fred Ward furniture 1959*

in the life of Canberra since the 1950s and how it had provided the attractive academic environment sought by the founders of Canberra and the University and enjoyed by their heirs and successors. Following his dismissal as Prime Minister in November 1975, Gough Whitlam lived for six months in one of the pleasant vice-chancellor suites at University House. Important works by noted Australian artists are integrated with the architecture and landscape, and the simple and elegant furniture designed by Fred Ward played a significant role in the development of the interior design and craft professions in Australia. University House has been described as one of the treasures of Canberra and there are now architects and other visitors to Canberra who will stay nowhere else.

In June 1995, we were invited to submit designs for a new 'link' building in the Linnaeus science precinct on the west bank of Sullivan's Creek. At the time, this was a quiet low-rise part of the University facing the residential colleges along the base of Black Mountain and boasting a considerable collection of rare specimen trees. Planning controls for the precinct required buildings to use 'brown-red dry pressed

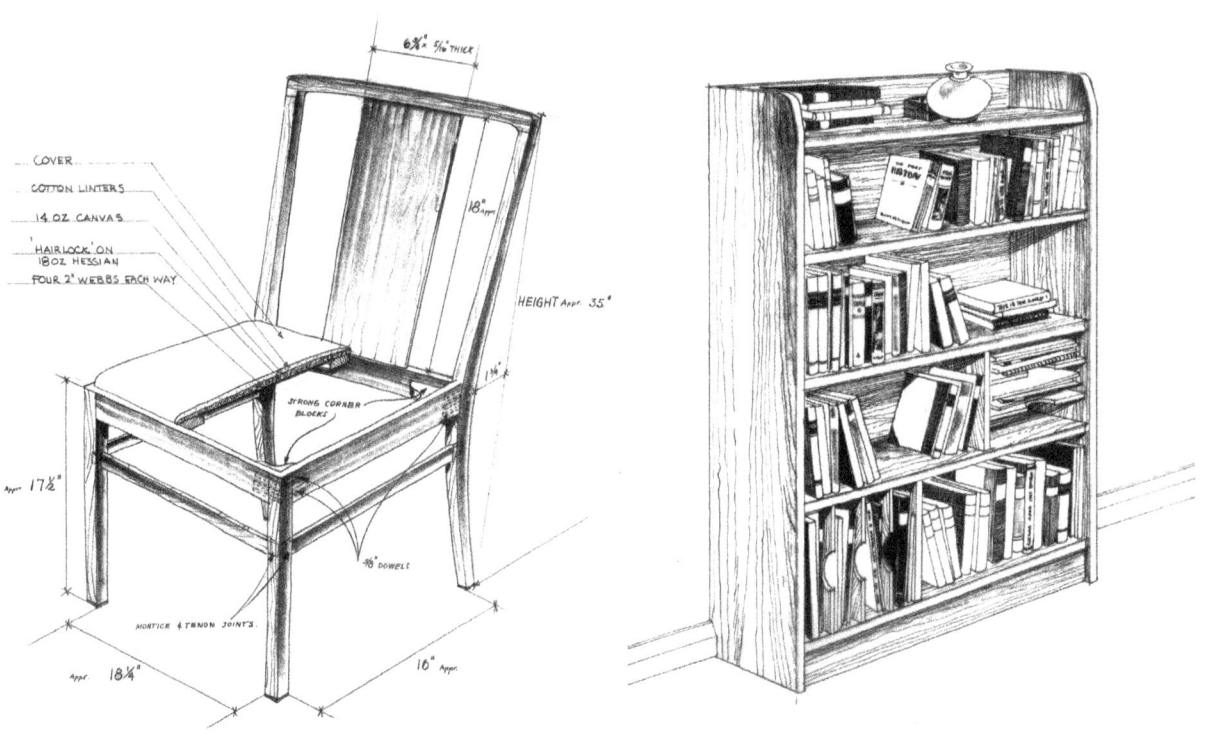

*Botany and Zoology competition model*

face brickwork with white joints and off-white rendered columns', a materials palette which combined with the plantings to make a pleasing streetscape and attractive external spaces. The Division of Botany and Zoology (known internally as BOZO) occupied two modest brick buildings on Daley Road, one of which was designed by Robin Boyd in 1963. The Boyd building had a chequered history with problems of water drainage, steelwork rectification and industrial accidents. 'To cap it off', said one report, 'a runaway Jaguar rolled down the embankment where it crashed through a wall of the building'. It sounded to me like a jinxed site, but we did not win the competition so we escaped a repeat of any such calamities. The teaser for us was that arrangements had been made by the University for the new building to be opened by David Attenborough. I worked with Ivo Tanevski in my office to develop an attractive and functional design that we hoped would have us stand alongside Attenborough at the opening, but to no avail. I never did get to meet Attenborough.

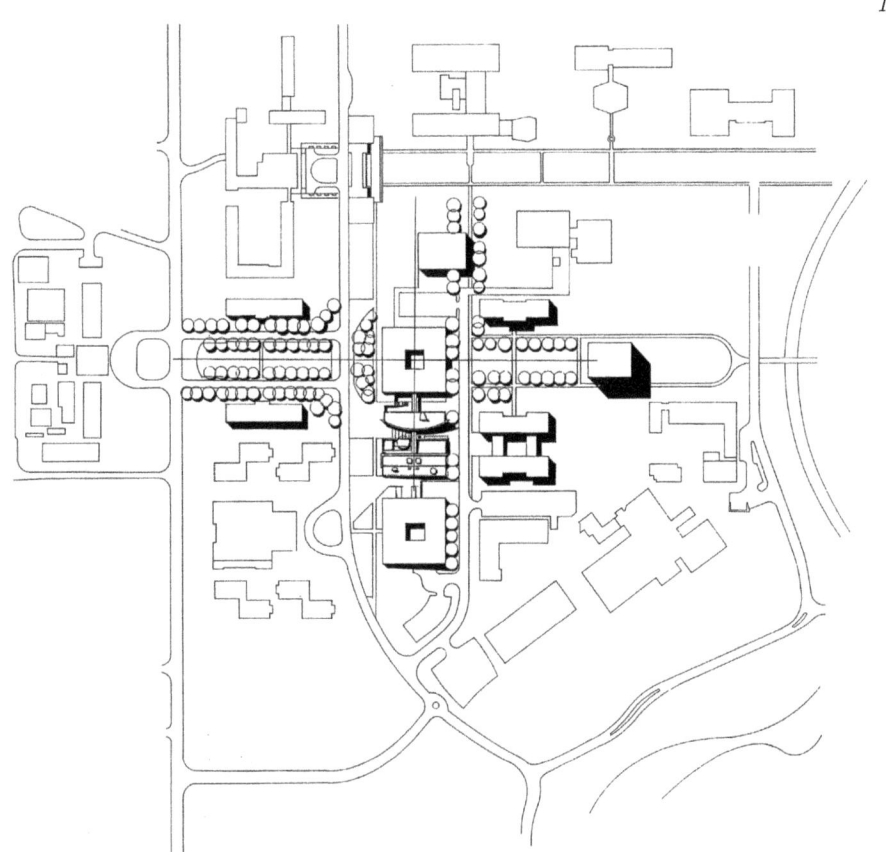

*The Australian National University Botany and Zoology competition 1995 site plan*

In 1994, we were invited to submit designs for a Vice-Chancellor's residence at the University of Canberra, a competition won by Romaldo Giurgola. Our submission proposed a main building in attractive gardens plus two detached studio apartments with private courtyards for visitors. I had stayed at several universities and diplomatic missions abroad and was acutely aware of the need for a formal but welcoming building that offered comfort and privacy for both hosts and guests. This was one of my most satisfying unrealised projects.

We entered further competitions with mixed success. Our entry in a 1991 urban design competition for the city foreshore of Perth suggested a physical framework for the long term regeneration of the Swan River frontage. A river axis parallel to the city grid from Mt Eliza and a new civic axis at right angles tied the river to the older city landmarks, forming a broad city domain from the river to a city square.

*Other Competitions*

*The Australian National University
Asian Studies Building 1994
competition drawing*

*University of Canberra
Vice-Chancellor's residence
model 1994*

At the intersection of the axes we built a new island and a lofty monument from which there would be views of the city and surroundings not previously available. We put a powerful laser beam on top of the monument and said that it could join China's Great Wall as a man-made object visible from the moon. We softened the city edge somewhat with a sandy beach to encourage the return of the wading birds which once used both land and river. We did not win the competition but our drawing was used as the cover image for a retrospective exhibition 'Take me to the River' in 2013.

We fared better in 1995 with our designs for a new building at the headquarters of the Therapeutic Goods Administration in south Canberra. New offices and laboratories were needed for three professional and technical divisions weighed down by conflicting opinions as to their relative importance and unwilling to work within sight of each other. We won the competition with

*Perth Foreshore competition 1991*

*Therapeutic Goods Administration Symonston 1995*

a new building which separated the warring parties by giving one side of a triangle to each. A central two-storey demilitarised zone is crowned by a shallow dome which was prefabricated in timber by a Queanbeyan boat builder and brought to the site very early on a Sunday morning. Tipped up on edge and taking a long and slow route, it looked as if a flying saucer had dropped in to visit. Television stations and newspapers had a good time filming what looked like an episode for Independence Day up Narrabundah Lane with roadblocks and police outriders. Our building sits comfortably on its semi-rural site and received a Master Builders Association Excellence in Building Award in 1997.

In 1998 we were invited to submit designs for the redevelopment of two blocks of land in Dickson leased to the ACT Totalisator Agency Board. We won the competition with a bullet-shaped building sporting a huge digital screen, which we said could be used to show horse races or the news of the day or whatever. Terry Snow, who was one of the judges, told me it was the best commercial solution and certainly the most interesting but it had been blackballed by the local roads and traffic authority who thought it would cause accidents because drivers on Northbourne Avenue (which was more than 200 metres away) would be distracted by moving pictures of horses. And that was the end of that. In due course the local government sold the

*ACTTAB redevelopment
Dickson ACT 1998
competition
del. Eddie Gonzales*

*The Melbourne Building*

*del. Eddie Gonzales*

*Belconnen Soccer Club*

Agency and the land has since been developed for a boilerplate apartment building.

The Sydney and Melbourne Buildings sit each side of Northbourne Avenue at its junction with London Circuit and were the first commercial developments in the civic centre of Canberra. The buildings have a wide ground floor colonnade and upper floor verandahs behind which have been a range of businesses including cafes, shops and banks, mostly built as individual premises of varying widths and depths. The bulk of the western half of the Melbourne Building was built by the Commonwealth in the early 1940s and was offered for sale by tender in the 1990s. This was the building that had burned down in 1953 not far from us at Canberra High School.

In 1997, Annabelle and I joined a consortium to buy the western half of the Melbourne Building with the intention of living in a New York style north-facing loft apartment on Alinga Street and with an income from two or three restaurants on the ground floor. One of the partners dropped out at the last minute and this dream was not to be. Instead, the building was purchased by Tim Efkarpidis, for whom I restored the façades and opened up the upper level balconies for an apartment hotel. We put an Irish pub on one corner and restaurants the length of West Row, bringing new life to an important remnant of Canberra's early history. Our surface scrapings of walls and windows revealed original paint colours and these were adopted as the heritage colour scheme for both the Sydney and the Melbourne Buildings. The project has been an outstanding commercial success and in 2001 received the Property Council of Australia Rider Hunt National Award for Innovation and Excellence.

Women's football was included in the Olympic Games for the first time at Atlanta in 1996. Canberra was a host city for women's football at the Sydney Olympics in 2000, with matches played at Bruce Stadium. Of the eight countries in the competition, all but Sweden played at least one game In Canberra. Practice facilities were provided by local football clubs including the Belconnen Blue Devils, whose field in Mackellar had been recently upgraded to international standards by Canberra engineer Ray Young. Without doubt the best pitch in town, it was reserved early on by the United States, who were the favourites for the gold medal but who were beaten in the final by Norway 3-2. There was a noticeable increase in support for soccer after the Games and I was asked to design a modest grandstand at the Mackellar ground with covered seating for 500 spectators.

The design provides an elevated 'street' for primary circulation with direct access to the press box and canteen and with various cantilevered platforms for television cameras. Below are change rooms for home and away teams, referees' rooms and other player facilities and storage. The expressed steel structure gives a pleasing rhythm and scale to the building, which is emphasised by the seating pattern and uplighting of the corrugated ceiling. The ground is now home to Canberra United in the W-League and has been adopted by the Matildas, Australia's national women's team, which has gone from strength to strength in recent years. I am a keen follower of women's football and go to the Belconnen ground regularly. When the grandstand is full and everybody is stamping their feet, it is quite an awesome place to be. The building received a Commendation from the Institute of Architects in 2003.

*Belconnen Soccer Club 2001*
Ben Wrigley

*Some Writings*

I have researched and published commentary and architectural critique in many areas of design and urban planning. I have an abiding interest in Canberra and the work of its early architects, preparing entries for the *Australian Dictionary of Biography* on Ken Oliphant and Cuthbert Whitley and later for Philip Goad and Julie Willis in their *Encyclopedia of Australian Architecture* with entries on John Overall, R C G Coulter and the National Capital Development Commission. The *Washington Times* published a lengthy article on the planning of Canberra in 2001 and I wrote an introduction ('The Dream of a Dreamer') for Andrew Metcalf's Watermark book *Canberra Architecture*. On behalf of the ACT Planning Authority I prepared guidelines for residential planning applications including a *Guide to High Quality Development in the ACT* and *Character Guidelines for Residential Core Areas of inner north and south Canberra*. I have particularly enjoyed the preparation of conservation management plans and associated architectural backstories for well-known local landmarks such as University House, the Old Patent Office by Cuthbert Whitley, St Christopher's School and Convent in Manuka by Roarty & Roarty and Harry Seidler's Trade Group Offices on Kings Avenue.

The centenary of Australian federation in 2001 was marked by infrastructure and tourism projects in each of the States and Territories. Melbourne, the seat of government of the Commonwealth for the first quarter of its life, ran a competition for a city square on the site of the old railway yards on Flinders Street. Canberra's centenary project was a National Museum of Australia on the Acton peninsula to be collocated with the Australian Institute of Aboriginal and Torres Strait Islander Studies. I worked happily for several months in 1997 with the Museum and AIATSIS and wrote the functional briefs for a two-stage design competition. Back to selling dreams, I suppose. Interestingly, both Melbourne and Canberra celebrated federation with breakthrough love-them-or-leave-them architectural statements.

In 2005, I worked with officers of the Department of Environment and Heritage in the preparation of the comparative analysis of the Sydney Opera House for nomination to the UNESCO World Heritage List. The justification for inscription describes the Opera House as 'an architectural masterpiece of human creative genius' with 'a great formal power and metaphorical richness that is uniquely appropriate to its cultural purpose and setting'. Praised as 'the youthful masterpiece of Denmark's most original and outstanding modern architect', the nomination of the Opera House was supported by architects and scholars all over the world and by Pritzker Prize winning juror Ada Louise Huxtable. Romaldo Giurgola said that Utzon's architecture 'transcends the mere art of building ... a poetic invention that has a strength and harmony not unlike the forms of nature herself'.

The nomination was successful and the Opera House was added to the World Heritage List in June 2007. Sydney then had a cultural monument of its own to match Melbourne's Royal Exhibition Building, which three years earlier became the first building on the Australian mainland to be given World Heritage recognition. Not surprisingly, Sydney was quick to say that justice had been done. Perhaps Canberra will one day complete the trifecta with its own architectural and cultural triumph, a building admired by all Australians and worthy of world heritage listing, a concert hall on Lake Burley Griffin perhaps?

*Houses and Housing*

Housing in all its forms is a major element in the garden city image of Canberra. Griffin's plans showed the gently sloping lands north and south of the river laid out as residential subdivisions for houses or garden flats in tree-lined streets with public parks and landscaped private gardens. These 'garden suburbs' would be healthy and comfortable places to live with easy access to business and commercial centres and to the foothills and open lands beyond. The Australian dream of the 'quarter acre block' assumed mythical proportions after the Second World War but has received much negative press recently in Canberra and elsewhere, by no means all deserved. Robin Boyd called suburbia 'a half-world between city and country' and the pejorative associations of the word 'suburban' remain today, suggesting not only remoteness from the centre of things but also ordinariness. Conversely, use of the word 'urban' implies being 'with it', in and of the town or city, full of energy, cool and discerning. Proponents of 'vibrant' city centres conveniently ignore the appeal of both the suburban hinterland or the inner low-rise neighbourhoods where many choose to live. Fortunately, suburbia has had its share of staunch defenders. Hugh Stretton said you don't have to be mindless or ultraconservative to choose to live in a suburban house—Patrick White did, he said, and likewise Thomas Keneally. Closer to home, so did Manning and Dymphna Clark.

Older city edge suburbs are desirable residential addresses under constant pressure for redevelopment at increased densities. Suburbs to the north of Canberra's city district are within walking distance of the University and many other significant destinations. I recall the distress of many in Canberra at the prospect of a new medium density residential landscape for these areas but this is the inevitability of all living cities. The earliest planning controls for redevelopment in areas such as Turner and Braddon were unimaginative and unhelpful, making nominal reference only to urban design quality and public amenity and requiring little more than the amalgamation of two or more residential blocks and a limit of three storeys in height. The new apartment buildings in these pleasant tree-lined streets were almost universally poorly sited and built with high-maintenance external finishes. A general lack of imagination produced mirror-reversed floor plans and windows facing all points of the compass.

Suburban redevelopment in Canberra remains a relatively new field in the construction industry. It attracts a broad range of builders who do not engage architects and landscape architects. The results have been disappointing in all parts of town and build quality is disturbingly poor. The government and its powerful planning agency must take positive steps to raise the standards of suburban redevelopment; these streets and landscapes are, after all, our twenty-first century expressions of how most of us want to live.

In 2001, I was approached by a respected family of local builders disappointed by the emerging streetscapes in the inner north and keen to find an architect for a new apartment building through an invited competition. The site in Macleay Street Turner was opposite Ken Woolley's Seventh Day Adventist church and the Lutheran National Memorial church by Frederick Romberg. We won the competition with strong support from the local community, who thought that my design promised to be 'chic and a bit of fun'. The building façade and silhouette are gently modelled and floor plans are simple with generous and usable private balconies and

*Turner apartments 2001*
Ben Wrigley

good natural light and ventilation. A long gentle driveway at one end of the site allows for service deliveries and garbage collection within the basement level and avoids the dangerous practice of basement ramps sloping down steeply from pedestrian sidewalks. The smart design, careful landscaping and the reputation of the builder ensured that the units sold easily. The project received an ACT Government High Quality Sustainable Design Award, an Excellence in Building Award from the Master Builders Association and in 2004 was the ACT Housing Industry Association Apartment Building of the Year.

*Margaret Morris house*

I have a continuing interest in designing houses which respond with some style to both the site and the occupants. The Margaret Morris House in Yarralumla is a compact cottage addressing what was at the time a relatively new challenge—residential downsizing in Canberra's southern suburbs. Margaret came to Canberra with her husband Bede Morris in 1958 when he took a position at the John Curtin School of Medical

Research. They settled with their family in Yarralumla in a house designed for them by Melbourne architects Yuncken Freeman (who also designed at the time the Civic Square and Canberra Theatre and the Chancery at the ANU) and they later bought a semi-detached cottage in nearby Musgrave Street as an investment.

When Bede died, Margaret found the family house and large garden too much to handle. The Musgrave Street site of 650 square metres was small by old Canberra standards but the new house satisfies all of Margaret's expectations for an attractive and comfortable townhouse in familiar surroundings. The plan is a model for smaller houses in older streets with a narrow frontage, enjoying access to both sunlight and daylight and with living and sleeping areas away from the street. Ceilings are high at three metres and living areas are on one level, with internal access to a garage at the rear of the site. A basement contains a rather splendid cellar filled with marvellous Australian and French wines. In 2003, the Morris House received a Commendation from the Institute of Architects and an Excellence in Building Award from the Master Builders Association.

After Elisabeth and Luke left home, Annabelle and I found that our much loved house in Forrest did not work well for just two people. We needed a more open plan, private for relaxation and entertainment but connected to its surroundings and within walking distance of parks and cafes. The house should have some self-contained accommodation for guests and a studio for a home business and be capable of modification to meet changing needs as we aged. We found a site on Euree Street in Reid within walking distance of Civic, Lake Burley Griffin and Anzac Parade and on the southern edge of the Reid Garden City Heritage Precinct. Reid is the largest of Canberra's garden suburbs and is entered on the ACT Heritage Register and included in the Register of the National Estate.

The two storey house meets all of our expectations with light and sun entering the house in a wonderful variety of patterns throughout the day. The lofty *piano nobile* has visual links to the street and rear garden

*Reid house ACT 2006*
Grahame Crocket

*Margaret Morris house*
*Yarralumla 2003*
Ben Wrigley

*Reid house 2006*
Matt Kelso

with flowing internal and external spaces for sitting and entertaining and generous dining areas. The external form flows from the plan and cross section and fits well within the local red brick and pebbledash streetscape. The street face is solid and secure and gives few hints of the open and transparent house it protects. The garden areas are well screened by mature trees and boundary plantings and are enjoyed in complete privacy with a raised timber boardwalk threaded between the trees and across a water garden. A structural steel frame gives freedom to relocate most walls in the house and service infrastructure is zoned to allow various permutations in use. An active local residents' association works to conserve the built and landscape qualities of the adjacent heritage precinct. We were amused but pleased when we were asked if our house could be included in their annual public tours. We were also delighted when the house was awarded the Institute's Canberra Medallion in 2006.

*Reid House 2006*
Ben Wrigley

# Postscript

Sir William Holford noted in his 'Observations' of 1958 that 'it will be of some importance to the development of Canberra that there should be more and more people who care, and care deeply, what it looks like and what it becomes as a town to live in'. At about the same time, George Molnar was reminding his students that a city reflects the people who created it. What sort of place do we want Canberra to be? Should it be like Zurich—'dignity and leisurely grace'—or something with a bit more zip? In any event it will certainly change over time. It should certainly be a thoughtful city set in an attractive and meaningful landscape but it does not have to be dull.

Griffin thought it important that the capital city have 'a liberality in public space' and that its buildings be designed with proper attention to size and scale. Northbourne Avenue is our long front driveway, the ceremonial entrance to the city. It deserves a parade of buildings of stunning design quality with a pleasing array of three-dimensional and photographable facades and silhouettes, not wall-to-wall faceless glass apartment blocks but proud destinations with carefully created forecourts and gardens and artful changes in setbacks and materials and audacity. The sixty metres width of Northbourne Avenue must not read as an anonymous traffic tunnel but as a grand boulevard full of life, with generous sidewalks and buildings and gardens talking to each other over their shoulders and across the roadway. Just dandy. That will show Australia that we are looking after our capital city and it will set the gold standard for our urban image. If we don't get Northbourne Avenue right now it will be many years before it can be done again.

Equally important, City Hill and the spaces within London Circuit at the end of Northbourne Avenue, which are currently used for car parking, should be reserved for a genuine and generous city square and an attractive and accessible public domain on top of City Hill. If we lose this land to buildings, no matter how beautiful or useful these may be, we will not find a sunny city heart elsewhere. Perhaps we can also find a better name for those parts of town officially known as 'City' but uncomfortably signposted as 'City Centre'. 'City Hill' has a good ring to it and makes geometric and symbolic sense, a place for the citizens of Canberra in a triumvirate with Capital Hill and Russell Hill.

There are no 'busy streets' in this part of town (except perhaps Bunda Street and Lonsdale Street) because we do not yet have enough people to fill them. We should nourish Canberra's own special qualities and character and not try to be like somewhere else. We can afford to wait for the glass to fill; people should come to Canberra because it is a very fine city, not because it is very big. And the quest to import 'vibrancy' is a dangerous distraction. People will come from near and far and gather in places they like and where they feel safe. What Jane Jacobs called 'the safety of the streets and the freedom of the city' will in due course bring us an appropriate helping of urban intensity and street markets and fiestas and fun. In the meantime we can do something about our terribly boring skyline and streetscape, where no space or imagination has been wasted on lanes and alleyways or forecourts with trees. We can also stop putting plant rooms and rubbish on roofs, there is no excuse at all for this.

There is evidence that market forces and community energy will in due course help Canberra's established residential districts look after themselves. They will need statutory support from time to time but minimum interference please as they renew themselves as modern urban villages. Newer residential communities on the fringe of town deserve work to guarantee the landscape infrastructure and attractive public parks upon which Canberra's garden city reputation has been built. The quest for affordable housing demands policy initiatives that

work, creative planning guidelines and new building types and, most critically, a fresh approach to land release. It is not the job of governments to prop up land prices and it is fatuous to suggest that banks and housing associations are unable to play a constructive part in such modern-day investments. Who will promote alternatives to oversized apartment blocks bristling with balconies, maybe smaller 'apartment houses'? Where are the pleasant streets of row houses found all over the world on narrow blocks with small front gardens and comfortable rear courtyards? Why are houses in the suburbs limited to two storeys and why do we put up with low ceilings and dependence on airconditioning? Has the solar fence outlived its relevance? Why no basement flats or modern-day six-packs?

The territory plan should be re-imagined with the bar raised considerably higher than at present and a firm hand is needed to reject plans to drop buildings the size of battleships into residential streets. Canberra deserves town planners who dream out loud. Business and community leaders should support our elected representatives and the bureaucracy when they fight for high quality buildings and public spaces and speak up about it strongly when they don't. More modern-day Medicis who have grown up in this city may emerge from a wider appreciation of the contribution of the Efkarpidis and Snow families and others. After all, Regent Street in London and the Crescent in Bath started off as speculative real estate investments. My good friend David Evans speaks with pride of the Royal Australian Air Force in which he rose to be Chief of the Air Staff, saying that the RAAF 'has class'. Canberra has class too and we should keep it that way.

Henry Adams, whose great-grandfather was the second President of the United States and whose grandfather was the sixth President, wrote in 1877 from an emerging Washington DC to his friend Charles Gaskell in Boston: 'One of these days this will be a very great city if nothing happens to it'. It is up to us to make sure that nothing bad happens to an unfinished Canberra.

'Griffin is dead! Long live Griffin!'

I remember the first time I climbed the slopes of Mount Ainslie 30 years ago. Standing at the top, with the strong Australian sun on my back, I was told that I would some day see laid out before me one of the world's great city plans. The view was splendid even then, but I imagine I was rather sceptical about ever seeing Griffin's formal pattern of landscape and buildings imposed on such a vast, dry and quiet countryside. It has taken 70 years to create, but most of Walter Burley Griffin's design is today there for all to see. Those who doubted that it would ever be, and those who did their best to destroy it, are now mostly gone. Canberra, and Griffin's plan, exist as an act of faith.

*Architecture Australia*
September 1983